John Dickson's *A Doubter's Guide to Jesus* is a unique resource. In a secular, ideology-driven age, it promises remarkably balanced, even-handed, fair-minded presentations of Christian beliefs about Jesus Christ—all deeply informed by the primary sources. I can't recommend this book enough.

TIMOTHY J. KELLER

Contemporary views of the person and mission of Jesus Christ are as varied as the kinds of faith that attach themselves to Christianity. From the somber Calvinists to the exuberant Word-Faith movement, practitioners of the Christian religious enterprise continue to find new and innovative ways of discovering the "Man from Nazareth." In this exuberantly joyful meditation, Dickson, honorary associate in the department of ancient history, Macquarie University in Sydney, Australia, gathers the many facets of Jesus' life and explores each as one would study the facets of a valuable diamond. How can one man be both friend and judge, both God and servant? The author draws on ancient histories and Judeo-Christian religious studies to present a compelling and readable account of the complex figure that millions call Savior and Lord. There is no agenda except to place Jesus Christ before readers in ways that inform and refresh, inspire and encourage. This is a wonderful book and is highly recommended for readers, indeed seekers, at all levels.

PUBLISHER'S WEEKLY

# A DOUBTER'S GUIDE TO JESUS

# A VERY SHORT INTRODUCTION

The aim of this book is to provide readers with an introduction to the major portraits of Jesus found in the earliest historical sources. I say "portraits" (in the plural) because our best information points not to a tidy, monolithic Jesus but to a complex, multi-layered, and, at times, contradictory figure.

Some might be troubled by this, fearing that plurality equals incomprehensibility or unreliability. Others take it as an invitation to do some rearranging for themselves, trying to make Jesus neater, more systematic, and digestible.

Then there are those—I admit to being one of them—who quite like the idea that after two millennia of spiritual devotion, and more than two centuries of modern critical research, we still cannot fit this figure into a single box. Jesus, it seems, is destined to stretch our imaginations, confront our beliefs, and challenge our lifestyles for many years to come.

If I have done my job properly, readers will find themselves (just as I do) both disturbed and intrigued by the images of Jesus found in the first sources.

# 1

## IMAGININGS:
### MAKING JESUS IN OUR IMAGE

Jesus the political rebel. Jesus the guru. Jesus the right-wing crusader. Jesus the left-wing activist. Jesus married-with-three-children-then-divorced. Jesus who never lived. Whether through misinformation, wishful thinking, or prejudice—and sometimes all three—the Jesus of public imagination is often markedly different from the figure we find in our earliest sources. Our assumptions prove misleading.

## THE JESUS OF PUBLIC IMAGINATION

When I say "public imagination" I include here the imagination of the Christian church. Although I write as a participant in mainstream Christianity (a boring Anglican, if you want to know), I am frequently struck by the difference between the Christ preached in some contemporary sermons and the man who emerges from the pages of history. I confess that somewhere deep inside my computer's hard drive are numerous sermons I have delivered in the past but, for reasons that will become clear in the following pages, I could no longer offer with sincerity and so will never preach again.

Equally questionable are some of the assumed Jesuses in popular discourse. We laugh now when we see those Hollywood blockbusters of the 1960s and 70s, such as *King of Kings* or *Jesus of Nazareth*. Jesus is transformed into a kind of peace-and-love California hippie, with beautiful things to say and sun-bleached blonde looks to boot. In the 1980s the controversial director Martin Scorsese gave us *The Last Temptation of Christ* in which the figure at the heart of Christianity is a sexually repressed prophet who isn't quite sure of his identity and mission.

Equally provocative was the 2003 Dan Brown novel *The Da Vinci Code*. In the story, experts effortlessly strip back the ecclesiastically conspired "Son of God" to reveal the true man—a simple, wise teacher who settled down with a wife and kids and whose descendants can be found living happily in modern France.

The next year Mel Gibson tried to redeem the task of popularly portraying Jesus with his $600 million box office success, *The Passion of the Christ*. Complete with dialogue in Aramaic and Latin, the languages of Jesus and the Romans respectively, Gibson wanted to tell the story of Jesus' trial and death in an authentic way. I admit, I was deeply moved by the film and found it realistic: those who criticised Gibson for "exaggerating" the sufferings of Christ forget that scourging and crucifixion were intentionally horrifying modes of punishment in the Roman world (more about that in chapter 10). Nevertheless, the Jesus that emerged from Gibson's portrayal was, despite the attempted realism, a one-dimensional figure. He was a mere sacrificial lamb. There is of course a truth here, as any first-year theology student will tell you, but it is a truth devoid of historical context and detached from the extraordinary life that preceded this suffering and gives it its proper meaning. My atheist friend had a point when he said that, without an appreciation of what Jesus said and did, watching the poor guy get beaten up for two hours was not spiritually enlightening.

## THE JESUS OF ACADEMIC IMAGINATION

Some *academic* images of Jesus are equally open to criticism. Readers may be surprised to learn that scholarly books and articles on the "historical Jesus" number in the tens of thousands. A vast industry has emerged in the last thirty years dedicated to uncovering the real Jesus—as opposed, it is thought, to the Christ of the church.

Typically, however, the only studies to attract public attention are the "sensational" ones—those that contradict mainstream perspectives on Christ. These studies hit the headlines and make their way into documentaries. The viewing public is left understandably perplexed, unaware that most of the best scholarship never reaches them.

I have explored this in detail in another book (*The Christ Files*), but it is worth repeating here. It is a sad fact of scholarship (in many academic fields) that the most impressive work is too subtle, cautious, and sophisticated (i.e., boring) to be considered newsworthy by the regular media outlets. The headline "Jesus Ate Meals with Sinners and Outcasts" is hardly going to excite a newspaper editor, even though it is based on solid data. The headline "Jesus Was Gay," on the other hand, will cause a small media storm, even if it is based on the musings of astrology! ("Jesus Was Gay, Says Academic," http://www.smh.com.au/articles/2003/05/29/1054177665090.html.)

This highlights something that is well worth knowing about the scholarly game. In any field of academia, especially in New

Testament studies it seems, scholarship tends to fall into three broad camps, or three points along a continuum. Somewhere out on the left-hand margin is skeptical scholarship. Experts here ply the scholarly craft in the service of nay-saying and hyper-skepticism. They relish offering new theories that call into question the results of broader scholarship. On the opposite margin is apologetic scholarship, where experts focus mainly on defending traditional Christianity from skepticism. They often take their cue, in fact, from skeptical scholarship. Like skeptical scholars, most apologists have good credentials, but they tend to bypass the normal process of academic review and publish directly for the public.

Between these two margins is what you might call mainstream or middle scholarship. This is where the majority of professional scholars are to be found. Mainstream scholars rarely hit the headlines or the shelves of popular bookstores, but they are regularly published in the hundred or so peer-reviewed journals dedicated to the subject area. This basically means that to get a research article published in a reputable periodical, the article must first be read and approved by at least two international scholars (not connected to the author). Only then will the research become part of the scholarly conversation.

On the whole, mainstream scholars are little interested in debunking or defending Christianity; they are neither staunch skeptics nor devout apologists. They just get on with the business of analysing the New Testament and related material in the way historians treat any other comparable historical source from the period: whether Caesar, Seneca, or Tacitus on the Latin side, or Plutarch, Epictetus, or Lucian on the Greek.

## THE APPROACH OF THE *DOUBTER'S GUIDE*

I have no delusions about where along this spectrum of scholarship my own little book lies: nowhere. This is not an academic work, and I do not wish to suggest to readers that what follows is a careful distillation of the current scholarly debate about Jesus. My goals and approach are quite different.

In what follows I intend to keep within the bounds of the mainstream. While I am personally sympathetic to the aims of apologetic scholars—to commend Christianity for the consideration of others—I have drawn almost nothing from them in writing this book. I have drawn little from skeptical scholarship, either.

At times this will mean I have to be circumspect about things I actually believe to be true. For instance, when I mention the unavoidable topic of Jesus' reported miracles, readers will notice that I make no attempt to *prove* Jesus did in fact heal the sick, restore the blind, and so on. This is not because I do not accept these things; it is simply because I think the historical sources are incapable of proving (or disproving) things like healings. In this, and many other instances, I find the assessment of mainstream scholars more realistic as a historical conclusion: While historians cannot say Jesus actually healed the sick, they can, and mostly do, say that Jesus did things that those around him believed to be miraculous. Whether or not you and I concur with this belief depends not on historical considerations but on philosophical assumptions (such as what we regard as possible in the universe). More about this later.

**BOOK NOTES**

Some readers may be eager for some examples of what I am calling "mainstream" scholarship on Jesus, volumes that avoid both Christian apologetics and arbitrary skepticism and have enhanced my own study of Jesus. Some of my favourites—which doesn't mean I agree with everything in them—include the following:

- Meticulous research is on display in the 800-page volume (half dedicated to footnotes) by Craig Keener, *The Historical Jesus of the Gospels*. Grand Rapids: Eerdmans, 2009.
- The scholarly "A-Z" for this topic with over 227 entries from 110 international scholars is Craig A. Evans, ed. *The Routledge Encyclopedia of the Historical Jesus*. London: Routledge, 2008.
- A superb volume on my favourite theme in historical Jesus studies (discussed in chapter 8) is by Craig Blomberg, *Contagious Holiness: Jesus' Meals with Sinners*. Downers Grove, IL: InterVarsity Press, 2005. (Blomberg has also written an excellent introduction to the Gospels as historical sources, *Jesus and the Gospels: An Introduction and Survey*. Nashville: Broadman & Holman, 2009.)
- Two breakthrough volumes on Jesus, highlighting the importance of oral tradition for the first Christians, are James D. G. Dunn, *Jesus Remembered*. Grand Rapids: Eerdmans, 2003; and Richard Bauckham, *Jesus and the Eyewitnesses: The Gospels as Eyewitness Testimony*. Grand Rapids: Eerdmans, 2006.
- Thoroughly balanced and reliable is the volume edited by Oxford University's Markus Bockmuehl, *The Cambridge Companion to Jesus*. Cambridge: Cambridge University Press, 2001.

- A scholar renowned for his sophisticated philosophy of history as applied to the New Testament is Jens Schröter, *Jesus of Nazareth: Jew from Galilee, Savior of the World*. Waco, TX: Baylor University Press, 2014.
- A volume that serves as a perfect textbook for Jesus is Gerd Theissen and Annette Merz, *The Historical Jesus: A Comprehensive Guide*. Philadelphia: Fortress, 1998.
- More skeptical than most about the detailed results of the historical study of Jesus but nonetheless compelling in his analysis of what is core to Jesus is Dale C. Allison, *Constructing Jesus: Memory, Imagination, and History*. Grand Rapids: Baker Academic, 2010.
- Equally cautious but no less important is E. P. Sanders, *Jesus and Judaism*. Philadelphia: Fortress, 1985.
- A tour de force over the last twenty years is the British bishop and biblical expert N. T. Wright, among whose key works is *Jesus and the Victory of God*. Philadelphia: Fortress, 1997.
- Four important Jewish contributions to the study of Jesus include David Flusser, *The Sage of Galilee: Rediscovering Jesus' Genius*. Grand Rapids: Eerdmans, 2007; Paula Fredriksen, *Jesus of Nazareth, King of the Jews*. New York: Vintage Books, 1999; Geza Vermes, *Jesus the Jew: A Historian's Reading of the Gospels*. London: Collins, 1973 (and Vermes's, *The Authentic Gospel of Jesus*. London: Penguin Books, 2003); and the fascinating Jewish commentary on some of Jesus' parables in Amy-Jill Levine, *Short Stories by Jesus: The Enigmatic Parables of a Controversial Rabbi*. San Francisco: HarperOne, 2015.

- A brief expert contribution to the topic is that by James Charlesworth, *The Historical Jesus: An Essential Guide*. Nashville: Abingdon, 2008.
- Finally, I want to recommend the works of two highly productive Australian experts: Michael Bird, *The Gospel of the Lord: How the Early Church Wrote the Story of Jesus*. Grand Rapids: Eerdmans, 2014; and Paul Barnett, *Finding the Historical Christ*. Grand Rapids: Eerdmans, 2009.

But this isn't just a book about history. Conscious of the evocative dimension of the figure of Jesus, I have tried throughout the book to give readers an idea of how these portraits of Christ have influenced church, society, and individuals, both ancient and modern. Each chapter ends with what I have called "Reflections." These should not be read as homilies designed to put readers on the spot. They are an attempt to highlight how both believers and unbelievers through the ages have found themselves confronted and/or inspired by these particular images of Jesus. While it is true that people have fashioned versions of Christ into their own digestible image, it is equally true that the figure of Jesus has exerted an enormous influence over those who have taken the time to ponder his life and teaching. I want to offer some insight into this more existential dimension of Jesus' story.

We begin with the obvious first question: How do we know what we know about Jesus? What are the sources, both direct and indirect, of our knowledge of the man?

# 2
## SOURCES:
### HOW WE KNOW WHAT WE KNOW ABOUT JESUS

Unlike the Hindu Upanishads, which focus on the believer's merger with the life force Brahman, or the Buddhist Tripiṭaka, which emphasises the extinguishment of self and suffering, or the Islamic Qur'an, which centres on the nature and practice of submission to God, the New Testament revolves around a series of events that are meant to have occurred in Judaea and Galilee between 5 BC and AD 30. This makes Christianity particularly open—some would say *vulnerable*—to historical scrutiny. The logic is simple: If you claim that something spectacular took place in history, intelligent people are going to ask you historical questions. Christianity has, on the whole, welcomed this. It is as if the Christian faith places its head on the chopping block of public scrutiny and invites everyone to take a swing. Thus far Christianity has fared well.

Jesus arrived on the scene at a time of great literary activity. Philosophers were writing weighty tomes on the meaning of life. Poets and playwrights were composing material to make people laugh and cry. Emperors were crafting royal propaganda to ensure they were well remembered. And historians were recording for posterity all that they could discover about the startling events surrounding the rise of the Roman Empire. The non-biblical writings from this period (100 BC–AD 200) fill many shelves at your local university library.

One lucky outcome of this flurry of ancient literary output is that a small-town Jewish teacher, named *Yeshua ben Yosef*, or Jesus son of Joseph, happened to rate a mention in several of the writings of the period. This is not as predictable as you might imagine. Although today we recognise Jesus as the founder of the world's largest religion, back in the first century he was hardly known at all outside the tiny strip of Roman-ruled land the Jews called Israel. It is a sheer and happy accident of history that Jesus rated a mention outside the texts of the New Testament (a selection of readings from these non-Christian sources can be found at the end of this chapter).

---

**BOOK NOTES** | In *The Christ Files: How Historians Know What They Know about Jesus* (Grand Rapids: Zondervan, 2010), I explore the sources and methods used by mainstream scholars to gain a plausible picture of the historical Jesus. A fuller account of the material in this chapter can be found there.

---

Our direct sources of information about Jesus come from three sets of ancient writings: Graeco-Roman, Jewish, and Christian.

# GRAECO-ROMAN REFERENCES TO JESUS

Jesus is mentioned in passing on numerous occasions in the writings of Greeks and Romans in the period following his death. The list includes the following:

1.  The pagan historian Thallos, around AD 55, in the third volume of his *Histories*, mentions a darkness coinciding with the crucifixion of Jesus. He describes it merely as a natural eclipse of the sun. His remarks were preserved by an ancient Christian named Julius Africanus, but not as a kind of proof of Jesus. Africanus only cites Thallos because he wants to take issue with the pagan historian's naturalistic explaining away of an event that Christians saw as a miracle.

2.  The stoic writer Mara bar Serapion, sometime after AD 70, refers to Jesus as a king, teacher, and martyr, and he compares him to the Greek greats Pythagoras and Socrates (who were also persecuted).

3.  The Roman historian Cornelius Tacitus (AD 56–120) scathingly refers to Jesus' execution under Pontius Pilate and describes the movement surrounding him as a "deadly superstition." This text is particularly important given Tacitus's reputation among contemporary historians as imperial Rome's greatest chronicler.

4.  The Roman administrator Pliny the Younger (AD 61–113) mentions the early Christian worship of Jesus "as a god." This may imply that Pliny knew Jesus was a mere man of recent memory but that his followers elevated him "as if" he was divine.

5. The Roman historian Suetonius, around AD 120, refers to disturbances among Roman Jews (of which there were thousands) over the claim that Jesus was the "Christ" (i.e., the Jewish Messiah). He gets the name slightly wrong, calling him "Chrestus," so a few modern scholars depart from the mainstream and suggest that the reference is not to Christ but to some other figure with a similar sounding name.

6. The Greek satirist Lucian of Samosata (AD 115–200) ridicules Jesus as a "crucified sophist" who taught people to "deny the gods." His work is a sustained mockery of a fraudster and one-time Christian named Perigrinus.

7. The Greek intellectual Celsus, around AD 175, insists Jesus' conception was suspect and his miracles mere Egyptian magic. Like Lucian, Celsus probably writes too long after Jesus to be regarded as good evidence for anything concerning him.

## JEWISH REFERENCES TO JESUS

Jesus is mentioned on four occasions in Jewish writings of the first and second centuries:

1. The first-century Jewish aristocrat and historian Josephus recounts Jesus' fame as a teacher, healer, and martyr. In one version of Josephus's text, Jesus' resurrection is said to have been "reported" by his followers. Much nonsense is written about this passage on the "skepti-net," with some claiming that experts usually dismiss Josephus's reference to Jesus as an insertion, or what's called an interpolation, by a later Christian copying out Josephus's works. In fact, virtually

all specialists today—whether Jewish, Christian, or of no faith—accept that Josephus did mention Jesus' fame as a teacher, healer, and martyr. The conclusion of the revered Oxford Jewish scholar Geza Vermes has stood the test of time: "Josephus deliberately chose words reflecting a not unsympathetic neutral stand . . . [B]y describing Jesus as a 'wise man' and 'performer of paradoxical deeds', Josephus achieved what few if any of his successors, ancient or modern, have done, namely that by neither approving nor disproving him, he managed to sketch a portrait of the Galilean master that is in a true sense *sine ira et studio* ('without resentment and devotion')." (Readers with access to a university library, online or in the real world, can access Vermes's now classical article "The Jesus Notice of Josephus Re-Examined," in *Journal of Jewish Studies* 38.1, 1987: 1–10.)

2. In another text the same writer recounts the martyrdom of a man called James, whom Josephus describes as the "brother of Jesus the so-called Messiah." The same brother, incidentally, appears frequently in the New Testament (Mark 6:3; Acts 12:17, 15:13; Galatians 1:19; James 1:1; Jude 1). There are no concerns about an interpolation with this passage.

3. The Talmud, an ancient exposition of Jewish law, contains a passage (which probably records a tradition of the early second century) justifying Jesus' execution at the time of the Jewish Passover on the grounds that he "led Israel astray" and "practised sorcery."

4. In a later text (post AD-200) the Talmud also insists that Jesus' mother Mary was an adulteress. The late date probably empties this reference of any importance.

## PIECING IT ALL TOGETHER

These Graeco-Roman and Jewish references provide little more than an outline of Jesus' life. They are too brief and cursory to be of value in reconstructing a "life of Jesus." Some of the passages were written too late to be of much historical value at all. Nevertheless, it is worth listing the handful of details about Jesus we can glean from non-Christian sources, without even opening a Christian text.

1. The name "Jesus."
2. The place and timeframe of his public ministry (Galilee and Judaea during Pontius Pilate's governorship, AD 26–36).
3. The name of his mother (Mary).
4. The ambiguous nature of his birth.
5. The name of one of his brothers (James).
6. His fame as a teacher.
7. His fame as a miracle worker/sorcerer.
8. The attribution to him of the title "Messiah/Christ."
9. His "kingly" status in the eyes of some.
10. The time and manner of his execution (crucifixion around the Passover festival).
11. The involvement of both the Roman and Jewish leadership in his death.
12. The coincidence of an eclipse at the time of his crucifixion.
13. The report of Jesus' appearances to his followers after his death (if the alternative version of the Josephus passage is accepted, which may be debated).
14. The flourishing of a movement that worshipped Jesus after his death.

Obviously, nothing can be gained from the above about what Jesus stood for, what he expected from his followers, or what drove him to the path of martyrdom. For these details we must turn to the third and most important direct source of information about Jesus: the writings of the New Testament.

## CHRISTIAN WRITINGS ABOUT JESUS

I once chatted to a highly intelligent woman who asked me about the sources of our knowledge of Jesus. I took her through the Graeco-Roman and Jewish sources. She was happy enough with those. I then began to list the Christian sources. She stopped me and said, "But surely you can't use those. They were all written by religious believers." She somehow got it into her head that religious devotion disqualified religious texts from being considered historical data as well.

Let me try to clear up two important misunderstandings about the writings of the early Christians. First, the so-called religious nature of Christian writings does not diminish their value as historical sources. It is true that historians take the Christian agenda into account when they analyse the New Testament writings, just as they do the biases in Tacitus and Josephus, but it is not the case that historians place Christian writings in a special category called "religion." Professional scholars approach the New Testament as they would any other first-century text. They do not treat it as the Word of God, as the Christian church does, but they do accord it the status of a valuable historical text. In fact, it is no exaggeration to say that historians (no matter what their persuasion) universally regard the New Testament writings as the earliest, most plentiful, and most important sources of information about the Jesus of history. One easy way to verify this is to open any major book on the historical Jesus and observe how the Graeco-Roman and Jewish sources just mentioned are treated in a matter of 10–20 pages (often less), but the New Testament texts provide the principal data for the remaining several hundred pages.

The second thing to say is that the New Testament is not a single source at all. It is a collection of sources. In the discipline known as "theology" (the study of God's nature and activity), the Bible is very appropriately treated as one unified source—all ultimately coming from God. Passages from one biblical writer are placed seamlessly next to passages from another in order to build up a coherent picture of the divine character and intentions. Sermons in church normally use Scripture in the same way. It is quite different in historical research. Historians analyse the New Testament as a compilation of independent traditions with common convictions about Jesus of Nazareth. Christians (especially) need to remember that, although the New Testament appears within a single volume today, complete with its own ISBN to prove it, originally these documents were composed and circulated independently of each other. They were not brought together into a "book" until the second, third, and fourth centuries.

## HISTORY NOTE

As the literature of the Christians grew, churches all around the Mediterranean decided to meet to discuss which texts were universally regarded as sacred and authoritative. A series of councils was called, climaxing in the councils of Rome (AD 382) and Carthage, North Africa (AD 397). The policy of these councils was highly conservative. Basically, they decided to embrace as Scripture only those documents that had long been recognised throughout the churches as penned by the first generation of Christian leaders, that is, by those whom Jesus appointed (Peter, Paul, James, etc.), or by their immediate colleagues (Mark, Luke, etc.). Thus, these councils culled rather than included, leaving us with just twenty-seven books of the New Testament (the Gospels and the letters). The other writings (e.g., Didache, Epistle of Barnabas, and others) were published in separate collections and are all readily available in English translations today. One of the most authoritative books on the question of how the New Testament documents came together was written by Bruce M. Metzger of Princeton University, *The Canon of the New Testament: Its Origin, Development, and Significance*. Oxford: Oxford University Press, 1997.

The apostle Paul, who wrote numerous documents now in the New Testament, never knew, for instance, the Gospel of Mark (and Mark never knew Paul's letters, either). Historians treat his epistles as a source separate from that of Mark. Again, the Gospel of John was composed (probably) independently of the Gospel of Matthew, so these individual Gospels represent another set of separate sources. James—the brother of Jesus mentioned earlier—did not know any of these Gospels, so his letter constitutes yet another source.

There are even sources *within* the Gospels, which historians treat as earlier independent traditions pulled together into a later text, in much the same way that Tacitus drew together prior sources in his famous Roman *Annals*. The Gospel of Luke, for instance, relies on at least three sources, according to most specialists today: (1) the Gospel of Mark written probably ten years before Luke; (2) a document dubbed "Q" (from the German *Quelle* meaning "source") that contained numerous sayings of Jesus; and (3) a source called "L" (the "L" stands for a source known uniquely to Luke), which was a collection of parables and other reports about Jesus. Luke himself in the opening paragraph of his Gospel mentions sources already known to him when he writes (in the AD 70s) and that he has researched for his own account of Jesus:

> Many have undertaken to draw up an account of the things that have been fulfilled among us, just as they were handed down to us by those who from the first were eyewitnesses and servants of the word. With this in mind, since I myself have carefully investigated everything from the beginning, I too decided to write an orderly account for you, most excellent Theophilus, so that you may know the certainty of the things you have been taught. (Luke 1:1–4)

Whatever else this is, it is a claim to be writing as a historian about historical events using prior historical sources. The modern identification of Luke's sources (as Mark, Q, and L)—though arrived at through other methods—is entirely consistent with what Luke himself affirms. Other recognised sources for the study of Jesus within the New Testament include "M" (a source known uniquely to Matthew); "SQ" (from the Greek *semeia* meaning "signs" and the German *Quelle* meaning "source," this is the so-called Signs

Source found within the Gospel of John); the letters of Paul; the epistle of James (the brother of Jesus).

To the general public, the fact that several parts of the New Testament say the same thing about Jesus does not seem all that significant. This is because most of us, if we ponder these things at all, are used to thinking about the New Testament as a single document. Historians view it differently. The fact that Paul, Mark, Q, and L independently offer strikingly similar descriptions of Jesus' life and teaching is highly significant. Because we are confident these sources were not copied from each other, we have to assume the information in these texts was both early and widely known. This is a basic principle of historical study. The *criterion of multiple attestation*, as it is known, affirms that when numerous ancient sources independently offer roughly the same information about an event or person, that information may be regarded as more plausible. It is the same logic you would apply to some surprising news from friends. If similar news came from two or three different friends, and you were confident they had not colluded, you would be far more likely to take them at their word.

## BACKGROUND SOURCES

So far we have been discussing direct sources about Jesus. There are also what you might call background sources. These are writings from the period that shed *indirect* light on the political, religious, and cultural context of Jesus' life. They provide the canvas on which our picture of Jesus can more realistically be painted. I will be drawing on many of these throughout the book.

1. The most obvious "background" source for the study of Jesus is the Tanak, or what Christians call the Old Testament. Historians are generally agnostic about whether Jesus fulfilled the Old Testament prophecies concerning a coming Messiah—as Christians affirm—but they do agree the Tanak provides one of the richest backgrounds for an accurate understanding of his message and conduct. We will meet the Old Testament many more times in this book.

## HISTORY NOTE

Tanak is an acronym for Torah (Law), Nevi'im (Prophets), and Ketuvim (Writings) and is the typical Jewish way of referring to the Scriptures that Christians call the Old Testament. Understandably, our Jewish neighbours are not keen on using the Christian terminology, since it could imply that their sacred writings are "old" or even redundant.

2. The famous Dead Sea Scrolls (found in caves near the Dead Sea between 1947 and 1956) provide a fascinating account of things like purity rules amongst certain Jews of Jesus' day. They say nothing directly about Jesus (most of the scrolls date from a century before Christ), but they do reveal, for instance, just how radical was Jesus' habit of striking up friendships with lepers, sinners, and women. Such things are frowned upon in the Dead Sea Scrolls.

3. The Mishnah is a collection of sayings of about 150 Jewish rabbis from the first and second centuries. When these words are set against the sayings of Jesus, we begin to get

a sense of how outrageous some of his teachings were in the eyes of his contemporaries. A striking example will be offered in the next chapter.

4. I have already mentioned the multivolume history of the Jews by Josephus. The main significance of these writings is not that they mention Jesus on two occasions but that they tell us much about the politics and culture of the time of Jesus. For instance, Josephus provides a wealth of information about the various anti-Roman resistance movements Jesus must have had in mind when he said things like "love your enemies" and "pray for those who mistreat you" (Luke 6:27–28).

5. The Pseudepigrapha contains sermons, novels, and letters written by Jewish leaders in the centuries before and after Jesus. One of the fascinating things they reveal is the kind of messiah some Jews in the period were hoping for. As we shall see in chapter 5, Jesus hardly fits the expected job description.

6. Roman writers such as Tacitus, Suetonius, Pliny, and Seneca all reveal the economic and political realities that Jesus and his fellow Jews had to endure in the first century. They also make clear why the Romans would have felt such contempt for the preposterous claim that a crucified Jew was the true Caesar of the world, a theme explored in chapter 11.

7. To these literary sources can be added the findings of archaeology. As you are reading this, scores of "digs" are going on all around the Mediterranean. Some of them are yielding important results for the study of Jesus. The discovery in 2009 of a first-century dwelling in Jesus' hometown of

Nazareth, for example, has enhanced our picture of the close-knit, traditional Jewish community in which he grew up. In the same year a synagogue was unearthed in Magdala, dating from the very time of Jesus—indeed, a coin with a precise date AD 29 (a year before Jesus' death) was found in the building. The discovery expands our knowledge of religious and educational life in the period.

8. The final background sources to mention are the so-called apocryphal gospels, works penned a century or more after the New Testament. These include the Gospel of Thomas, the Gospel of Philip, the Gospel of Mary Magdalene, and many others. I mention these here not because they provide any background information about the Jesus of history, but because in recent years it has become popular to suggest that the four New Testament Gospels (Matthew, Mark, Luke, and John) were officially accepted only very late in history and that various other Gospels were secretly excluded, all for devious political reasons. Something like this was described in Dan Brown's *The Da Vinci Code*. In reality, the four New Testament Gospels are the only Gospels we can be confident were written in the first century—the century when Jesus himself lived. But these writings unwittingly spawned a virtual Gospel-writing industry in the second and third centuries. As Christianity spread throughout the Mediterranean world, various splinter groups began to imitate, extend, and sometimes re-write the older teachings of Jesus. These groups produced their own Gospels in the names of former biblical greats (like Thomas, Philip, Mary Magdalene, and so on). That way, they could mount a claim

that Jesus himself had taught their idiosyncratic views. With very few exceptions, today's historians treat these extra "Gospels" not as sources for our knowledge of the historical Jesus but as testimony to the variety of responses to the figure of Jesus a century or two later.

Taken together, these direct and indirect, Christian and non-Christian sources provide (with the exception of the apocryphal Gospels) a wealth of information about Jesus Christ. The picture that emerges from the data, as I hope to show throughout this book, is both deeply credible and profoundly counterintuitive. It all strengthens the impression that the New Testament Gospels, the principal sources of our knowledge of the historical Jesus, are genuine historical documents, not legends, myths, or parables about the spiritual life. While forty to fifty years ago it was common to treat the Gospels as religiously valuable but historically questionable, today a consensus of secular scholarship affirms the Gospels as important historical writings. Jens Schröter of Humboldt University in Berlin is a recognised leader in the field, and no Christian apologist. He sums up well the mood and trajectory of contemporary scholarship on Jesus and the Gospels:

In recent research one can discern a clear tendency to grant the Gospels the status of historical sources, thus to view their Jesus narratives—beyond the faith convictions that undoubtedly come to expression in them—as also relevant in historical perspective. This signifies a turning point in Jesus research to the extent that they were denied this status for quite some time. The judgement that the Gospels are ultimately unfruitful for a historical presentation of the activity of Jesus due to their kerygmatic [i.e., "preachy"] character or their literary presentation can, however, no longer convince. Instead, they are perceived as narratives that are interwoven in diverse ways with the underlying events of the life and fate of Jesus of Nazareth. (Jens Schröter, *From Jesus to the New Testament: Early Christian Theology and the Origin of the New Testament Canon*. Translated by Wayne Coppins. Waco, TX: Baylor University Press, 2013, 96.)

What Schröter puts in his restrained and scholastic—dare I say *Germanic*—way can be restated simply: specialists now believe the Gospels provide a clear and invaluable window into a genuine first-century life. The rest of my book will hopefully bear out that important conclusion.

---

**BOOK NOTES**

There are so many good books on Jesus it is hard to recommend just one or two. I have often said to my students that the field of historical Jesus is so vast, to get a good sense of what most experts today think about Jesus you either have to read a minimum of twenty of the hundreds of important scholarly texts on the topic (I offered just such a list of twenty at the end of chapter 1) or sit through a university unit designed to introduce the entire field. But there might be a third way: Read one deliberate summary of the field by a noted scholar writing for the general public. I can think of only two such books, both published by Oxford University Press (OUP). One is Graham Stanton's *The Gospels and Jesus*, 2002. The other is Richard Bauckham's *Jesus: A Very Short Introduction*, 2011. The second book is just 144 pages and forms part of an extraordinary gift in modern publishing. Oxford University Press now has something like 500 volumes in the Very Short Introduction series, all of them written by leading scholars in the relevant field—whether the French Revolution, the Mongols, Marx, Atheism, Jesus, or whatever—but designed to give the general public a fast and reliable introduction to complex subjects. Its advantage over, say, Wikipedia is that readers are guided by an expert to understand what are the "mainstream" views in a field and what are "fringe" views. Often this distinction is lost in Wikipedia entries, where mainstream and fringe views end up getting equal weighting. This can end up being quite misleading, especially on a topic like Jesus.

Let me close with three brief reflections.

# REFLECTIONS

## The Nature of Christian Scripture

There is something quite instructive in all this about the distinctive nature of the Christian New Testament when compared with the Scriptures of other world faiths. The Islamic holy book, the Qur'an, for instance, is said to be a direct revelation from God entirely devoid of human participation in its composition. It is believed to be a perfect copy of the "Mother Qur'an" stored in heaven. The prophet Muhammad simply recited what was divinely dictated to him (*qur'an* means "recitation"). Likewise, the earliest and most sacred portion of the Hindu Scriptures, called the Vedas (from the word for "wisdom"), are believed to have been eternally and divinely disclosed without any human influence on the form or content of the revelation.

Christian Scripture is quite different. The books of the New Testament have always presented themselves, in the first place, as *historical* texts. They are biographies based on earlier sources and letters written to specific social settings. Does this observation undermine the Christian belief that the New Testament is also the Word of God? Not at all. From the very beginning, Christians treated their sacred documents as simultaneously human and divine. Just as Christian theology has had no problem thinking of Jesus as both God and man, so the church has (usually) had no hesitation affirming the New Testament as both a divinely inspired text and a truly historical text. Christianity is a historical faith based not on a divine dictation or private revelation immune from secular testing but on public events that are, for better or worse, open to public scrutiny.

## Christian Confidence

Christians often take the front foot on questions of the credibility of Jesus and the writings of the New Testament. Although they sometimes go too far—there is a fine line between confidence and arrogance—they are right to insist that after two centuries of modern critical scrutiny the basic plot of Christ's life recounted in the Gospels holds firm.

While media services will occasionally report "never-before-revealed Gospels" and late-night TV documentaries will sometimes purport to uncover the "real origins" of Christianity, none of this is likely to trouble informed Christians. When confronted by such media claims, many modern believers will respond by asking for the actual argument or evidence thought to challenge their beliefs. Christianity has been around far too long and has been assessed by far too many critics to make the average thoughtful Christian overly concerned about rumours of "new evidence." This is not to say new evidence may not be found in the future. The historical nature of Christianity means that it must always remain open to this possibility. My point is simply that Christian confidence is more solidly grounded than many outside the church often realise.

To Christians reading this I would like to add a caveat. By all means, take the front foot in matters of the historical basis of Jesus, but do so humbly and graciously. As the New Testament itself urges: "Always be prepared to give an answer to everyone who asks you to give the reason for the hope that you have. But do this with gentleness and respect" (1 Peter 3:15). Christian faith is well grounded, but it is not provable in a mathematical sense and it should never inspire smugness. Modern believers should never treat skeptics with disdain for doubting the claims about Christ.

## Reading Jesus Seriously

I hope you will not mind my adding a personal challenge that arises from this discussion. I would love to think that this book will help you explore the Gospels with the same mental discipline you would give to important documents from your own favourite field—law, sports, medicine, carpentry, finance, retail, education, music, language, or whatever. We do not need to become experts, and Bible reading doesn't have to be arduous. But readers of the

Gospels really should apply themselves to understanding the man from Nazareth with the same seriousness and attention to detail they would give to any other crucially important aspect of professional or personal life. A childlike "Sunday school" understanding of Jesus will be no match for the doubts of a thoughtful adult today. But a grown-up understanding of the man from Nazareth has proved stimulating and satisfying to some of the greatest minds of history and our day.

## A SELECTION OF READINGS FROM ANCIENT NON-CHRISTIAN SOURCES

### Tacitus (AD 115): Jesus and His Deadly Superstition

But neither human help, not imperial munificence, nor all the modes of placating Heaven, could stifle scandal or dispel the belief that the fire had taken place by order. Therefore, to scotch the rumour, Nero substituted as culprits, and punished with the utmost refinements of cruelty, a class of men, loathed for their vices, whom the crowd styled Christians. Christus, the founder of the name, had undergone the death penalty in the reign of Tiberius, by sentence of the procurator Pontius Pilatus, and the pernicious superstition was checked for a moment, only to break out once more, not merely in Judaea, the home of the disease, but in the capital itself, where all things horrible or shameful in the world collect and find a vogue. First, then, the confessed members of the sect were arrested; next, on their disclosures, vast numbers were convicted, not so much on the count of arson as for hatred of the human race. And derision accompanied their end: they were covered with wild beasts' skins and torn to death by dogs; or they were fastened on crosses, and, when daylight failed were burned to serve as lamps by night. (Tacitus, *The Histories and The Annales*. Translated by Clifford H. Moore, John Jackson. Loeb Classical Library. Cambridge: Harvard University Press, 1999, 15.44.)

## Governor Pliny's Letter to Emperor Trajan (AD 110): Christ As "God"

> For the moment this is the line I have taken with all persons brought before me on the charge of being Christians. I have asked them in person if they are Christians, and if they admit it, I repeat the question a second and third time, with a warning of the punishments awaiting them. If they persist, I order them to be led away for execution; for, whatever the nature of their admission, I am convinced that their stubbornness and unshakeable obstinacy ought not to go unpunished . . . I considered that I should dismiss any who denied that they were or ever had been Christians when they had repeated after me a formula of invocation to the gods and had made offerings of wine and incense to your [Emperor Trajan's] statue, and furthermore had reviled the name of Christ: none of which things, I understand, any genuine Christian can be induced to do . . . [T]he sum total of their guilt or error amounted to no more than this: they had met regularly before dawn on a fixed day to chant verses alternately among themselves in honour of Christ as if to a god, and also to bind themselves by oath, not for any criminal purpose, but to abstain from theft, robbery and adultery, to commit no breach of trust and not to deny a deposit when called upon to restore it. . . .
> (Pliny the Younger, *Letters*, Volume II, Books 8–10. Translated by Betty Radice. Loeb Classical Library 59. Cambridge: Harvard University Press, 1969, 10.96.)

# Josephus (AD 80s–90s): Jesus the Teacher, Martyr, and Christ

And so he [Ananus the High Priest] convened the judges of the Sanhedrin and brought before them a man named James, the brother of Jesus who was called the Christ, and certain others. He accused them of having transgressed the law and delivered them up to be stoned. Those of the inhabitants of the city who were considered the most fair-minded and who were strict in observance of the law were offended at this. (Josephus, *Jewish Antiquities, Volume IX: Book 20.* Translated by Louis H. Feldman. Loeb Classical Library 456. Cambridge, MA: Harvard University Press, 1965, 20.200.)

About this time there lived Jesus, a wise man. For he was one who wrought surprising feats and was a teacher of such people as accept the truth gladly. He won over many Jews and many of the Greeks. When Pilate, upon hearing him accused by men of the highest standing amongst us, had condemned him to be crucified, those who had in the first place come to love him did not give up their affection for him. And the tribe of the Christians, so called after him, has still to this day not disappeared. (Josephus, *Jewish Antiquities* 18.63–64.)

# 3

## TEACHER:
### HIS WORDS AND THEIR IMPACT

It is hard to imagine a more obvious statement about Jesus than that he was *a teacher*. Many of his sayings have become proverbial in English, used regularly without any remembrance of where they come from: "salt of the earth," "love thy neighbour," "do unto others," "the good Samaritan," "prodigal son," "blind leading the blind," "judge not, lest you be judged," "the one who lives by the sword, dies by the sword," "wolves in sheep's clothing," "cast the first stone," "eat, drink, and be merry," "sign of the times," "go the extra mile," and so on. Recently, I met with an Australian politician who explained how he has "always tried to live by the famous John F. Kennedy quotation, 'To the one who has been given much, much is required.'" He was surprised—and delighted—to learn that JFK got it from Jesus!

## MISTAKEN JESUSES

But there are two equal and opposite mistakes people make when thinking about the man Jesus. The first is made by the general public, the second by Christians.

Probably the most enduring image of Jesus in contemporary society is that of a teacher. If he is thought of at all, he is viewed as the archetypal wise man, someone who left behind great words to follow, a kind of Gandhi-figure. This was brought home to me powerfully when I took part in a discussion about Jesus some years ago on Triple J radio, the young and hip station of Australia's national broadcaster. The last twenty minutes of the show was talkback. Callers were invited to ring in and tell us what they thought of Jesus, or ask me any questions. I braced myself for the worst. To my delight, every caller—and there must have been ten—liked Jesus. What the callers especially appreciated were his teachings, the way he critiqued religious authority, demanded peace, and preached love and tolerance toward all classes of people. We could, in fact, have been talking about Gandhi!

None of the callers mentioned Jesus' healings or his claim to be the Messiah, God's Son. There was nothing about his death on the cross or reported resurrection to life. Jesus *the teacher* was the only thing on the table.

This is the first mistake people make in assessing Jesus: They so magnify his role as teacher that they end up diminishing, or ignoring altogether, some of the most striking and indispensable features of the Jesus of history. The result is a truncated Jesus, a Jesus of my preference and imagination.

This singular emphasis in our culture on Jesus as a teacher can be traced to the French philosopher and historian Joseph Ernest Renan (1823–92), who published his *Life of Jesus* in 1863 to much acclaim. Renan stripped Jesus of theological grandeur and cast him as a charming moral teacher whose morality was so strict he lost popularity and was eventually rejected. You have probably never heard of Renan, but his idea entered our world as a cultural "meme" that is now very popular. Experts today, however, think of Renan's portrait of Jesus as one-dimensional. It is a classic example of projecting our own values onto a historical figure. As a philosopher of the Enlightenment, Renan fashioned his "preferred" Jesus: a teacher of humanist values.

Equally flawed is the Christian (especially Protestant) overreaction to the general public's Teacher-Jesus. In seeking to affirm his climactic role as the Saviour who died and Lord who rose again, some in the modern church so downplay his role as teacher that he becomes almost unrecognisable as the Jesus of the Gospels, the Jesus of history. The conviction that he is *more* than a teacher can lead to the practical conclusion that he is *hardly* a teacher at all. The teachings recorded throughout the middle chapters of the Gospels come to be thought of as a mere precursor to the real ministry of Christ recorded in the final chapters.

Even at theological college we were frequently told that almost a quarter of each of the four Gospels is given over to describing Jesus' death and resurrection. Mark's Gospel, in particular, was described to us as a "Passion narrative with extended introduction." It was not until years later that it dawned on me: If 25 percent of each Gospel is concerned with Jesus' death and resurrection, this means 75 percent is concerned with his life and teaching!

I certainly want to affirm that Jesus' death and resurrection are presented in the earliest Christian sources as his crowning achievements, and I will have a lot more to say about these in chapters 9 and 10. All I am saying at this point is that, although Jesus was more than a teacher, he nevertheless *was* a teacher.

Historically speaking, Jesus' fame as a teacher is one of the most prevalent themes of the ancient sources.

**BOOK NOTES**

A superb summary article (of just seven pages) about Jesus' historical role as teacher was written by the German specialist from Dortmund University, Rainer Riesner, "Teacher, Teaching Forms, and Styles." *The Routledge Encyclopedia of the Historical Jesus.* Edited by Craig A. Evans. London: Routledge, 2008, 624–30.

## JESUS AS TEACHER OUTSIDE THE GOSPELS

Everywhere in our sources Jesus appears as a teacher of great influence. Even our non-Christian sources refer to his effect as a teacher—for good or ill.

Mara bar Serapion (sometime after AD 70), a pagan father writing home to his son, compares Jesus to the great Greek philosophers Socrates and Pythagoras, whose teachings continue on in the world long after their deaths: "For what advantage did the Athenians gain by the murder of Socrates . . . or the people of Samos by the burning of Pythagoras . . . or the Jews by the death of their wise King? . . . Socrates is not dead, because of Plato; neither Pythagoras, because of the statue of Juno; nor the Wise King, because of the laws which he promulgated" (The Epistle of Mara, Son of Serapion, 4.30–5.7. Translated by William Cureton. *Spicilgegium Syriacum: Containing Remains of Bardesan, Meliton, Ambrose, and Mara Bar Serapion.* London: Rivingtons, 1855,

73–74.) The first-century Jewish historian, Josephus, said a similar thing: "About this time there lived Jesus, a wise man. For he was one who wrought surprising feats and was a teacher of such people as accept the truth gladly. He won over many Jews and many of the Greeks" (Josephus, *Jewish Antiquities* 18.63).

Mara and Josephus offer a somewhat neutral description of Jesus as teacher. The ancient Talmud, an exposition of Jewish law, puts things in thoroughly negative terms: Jesus "enticed and led Israel astray" (bar. Sanhedrin 43a). This is a way of saying that Jesus influenced the nation more than the elites would have liked.

## JESUS AS TEACHER IN THE GOSPELS

An even clearer portrait of Jesus as a teacher is found in the Gospels. The first year of his ministry is summarized as, "Jesus went through all the towns and villages, teaching in their synagogues, preaching the good news of the kingdom" (Matthew 9:35). And, after his arrest three years later, he describes his ministry of those final weeks in very similar terms: "Am I leading a rebellion, that you have come out with swords and clubs to capture me? Every day I sat in the temple courts teaching, and you did not arrest me" (Matthew 26:55).

People also routinely called him a teacher. By my count, in direct speech people address Jesus simply as "Teacher," the way you might say "Sir," no fewer than thirty-one times. My favourite example is in the Gospel of Mark. In the middle of a terrifying storm on the Sea of Galilee (known for occasional rough weather) we find Jesus asleep and the disciples in a panic: "Jesus was in the stern, sleeping on a cushion. The disciples woke him and said to him, 'Teacher, don't you care if we drown?'" (Mark 4:38).

I suspect a Christian who regularly referred to Jesus as "Teacher" might be viewed a bit strangely in church circles. For some reason, it is just not part of ecclesiastical vocabulary anymore. I sometimes feel I should reintroduce it and see how it goes. At this point, the general public's over-emphasis on Jesus as a teacher offers something of a corrective to the church's forgetfulness.

Jesus referred to himself as "Teacher." The point is forcefully made in Matthew 23:8–10, where Jesus says to a crowd of his followers:

> But you are not to be called "Rabbi," for you have only one Teacher and you are all brothers. And do not call anyone on earth "father" [in the religious sense, that is], for you have one Father, and he is in heaven. Nor are you to be called "instructors," for you have one Instructor, the Messiah. (Matthew 23:8–10)

As it turns out, the first Christians did go on to address certain church officials as "teachers" (James 3:1; Ephesians 4:11). But this was only after a significant re-think of what the activity involved. The teacher's role in early Christianity was to memorise and pass on Jesus' words and deeds. Teachers were not fountains of the collective wisdom of hundreds of rabbis; they were more like repositories, or memory banks, for the wisdom of just one true teacher. As Professor James Dunn of the University of Durham explains:

Teachers, indeed, seem to have been the first regularly paid ministry within the earliest Christian movement. Why teachers? Why else than to serve as the congregation's repository of oral tradition [memorised accounts of Jesus]? . . . All who read these pages will have been bred to a society long accustomed to being able to rely on textbooks, encyclopaedias, and other reference works. But an ancient oral society had few if any such resources and had to rely instead on individuals whose role in their community was to function . . . as "a walking reference library." (Dunn, *Jesus Remembered*, 176–77.)

Teachers in early Christianity viewed themselves as the "walking reference libraries" of the one true Teacher, Jesus.

## THE CHALLENGE OF JESUS' TEACHING

This emphasis in the Gospels on Jesus as the one true Teacher highlights the serious challenge he posed to the teachers of his day. He consistently set his teaching against the traditions of the rabbis of Israel. And the crowds knew it. At the end of Jesus' famous Sermon on the Mount recorded throughout Matthew chapters 5–7 we are told:

When Jesus had finished saying these things, the crowds were amazed at his teaching, because he taught as one who had authority, and not as their teachers of the law. (Matthew 7:28–29)

This is a very revealing statement, historically speaking. Matthew is not simply saying that Jesus was rhetorically more effective than the "teachers of the law." His mention of "authority" here is a reference to the chain of authority the rabbis of the first century were commissioned to preserve. Virtually all Jewish teaching in this period involved listing the memorised rulings of former teachers on various ethical and legal matters. The authority of any given "teacher of the law" consisted in his ability to draw upon the vast body of collective rabbinic wisdom.

The most important of these rabbinic teachings were eventually compiled in the second holy book of Judaism, the Mishnah—still regarded as Scripture by Orthodox and Conservative Jews. The Mishnah, as I said in chapter 1, records the sayings of over 150 famous rabbis (from 50 BC—AD 200), organising them into sixty-three subcategories. My copy runs to 1100 pages. When Matthew's Gospel says here that Jesus "taught as one who had authority, and not as their teachers of the law," the writer means that Jesus cut right across the usual chain of rabbinic authority. Jesus rejected it as a man-made edifice that obscured rather than clarified the will of God.

The ancient topic of hand washing provides a good point of comparison between the teaching of Jesus and the teaching of some of his contemporaries. One section of the Mishnah is called Yadayim ("hands"). It is an eight-page summary of the correct way to wash one's hands before eating a meal. Ritual washing was an important part of ancient Judaism:

> The hands are susceptible to [spiritual] uncleanness and are rendered clean up to the wrist. How so? If one poured the first water [of two compulsory cleansings] up to the wrist, and the second beyond the wrist and it went back to the hand—it

is clean. If he poured out the first and the second pouring of water beyond the wrist and it went back to the hand, it is unclean. If he poured out the first water onto one hand, and was reminded and poured out the second water on to both hands, they are unclean. If he poured out the first water on to both hands and was reminded and poured out the second water on to one hand, his hand, which has been washed twice, it is clean. If he poured out water on to one hand and rubbed it on the other, it is unclean. (Mishnah Yadayim 2:3)

Jesus rejected many of these purity rules, describing them as man-made traditions that distorted the wishes of the Almighty. In the Gospel of Mark we catch Jesus in full flight on the theme of "hands":

So the Pharisees and teachers of the law asked Jesus, "Why don't your disciples live according to the tradition of the elders instead of eating their food with defiled hands?" He replied, "Isaiah was right when he prophesied about you hypocrites; as it is written: 'These people honor me with their lips, but their hearts are far from me. They worship me in vain; their teachings are merely human rules.' You have let go of the commands of God and are holding on to human traditions." (Mark 7:5–8)

For Jesus, what mattered was not the ethical artifice constructed by society—his or ours—but the direct will of God that he, as the one Teacher, claimed to embody.

# THE HEART OF JESUS' TEACHING

What was the heart of Jesus' teaching? Was he a theologian, a moralist, a philosopher, or something else?

Bestselling author and social analyst Hugh Mackay recently published *Beyond Belief.* The book presents a thoughtful, culturally informed argument to the effect that we do not need religion in order to maintain either a sense of meaning or an "ethic of love": we can happily move *beyond belief.* I have many questions about his central thesis, but I am particularly interested in what he says about Jesus. It is unusual that an Australian public intellectual would have anything to say about Jesus, so I was delighted that Mackay would raise the topic. His conclusions, however, are different from my own.

Throughout the book Mackay is keen to sever any necessary connection between the good life and religion. In a section titled "What Did Jesus Actually Teach?," he takes readers on a tour through Jesus' parables and the content of the famous Sermon on the Mount. He then concludes:

> None of the explicit teachings of Jesus, in the parables or in that sermon, called on his disciples to *believe* anything. He was not prescribing doctrine or dogma for some hypothetical institutional church that might in the future have been established in his name. His teachings were *all* about how best to live: the consistent emphasis was on loving actions, not belief. (Hugh Mackay, *Beyond Belief.* Macmillan Australia, 2016, 230–31; emphasis original.)

In various lectures and interviews promoting the book, Mackay put it even more succinctly: "Jesus never told anyone what to believe in. He only spoke about how to treat each other."

I will reflect on how fair Mackay's assessment is in a moment. But the other interesting thing he does in the book is relativise one of Jesus' most famous teachings, the so-called Golden Rule: "Do to others as you would have them do to you." Again, in an effort to distance such ethical insights from any necessary religious outlook, Mackay informs readers that the Golden Rule is a universal human principle: "There is nothing remarkable in this: virtually every religious and philosophical tradition on earth promotes the same idea" (237). He offers for comparison the well-known saying of Confucius, the great Chinese intellectual and moralist of the fifth century BC, who taught, "Do not inflict on others what you yourself would not wish done to you" (Confucius, *The Analects*. Translated by D. C. Lau. Penguin Classics. London: Penguin Books, 1979, 15.24). Grammatically, there is great resonance between the saying of Jesus and the teaching of Confucius. But the parallel is in form rather than substance. What Jesus states positively Confucius frames negatively. One is about doing the good to others that you would like to experience yourself. The other is about refraining from doing the harm you don't want to endure yourself. Both are excellent pieces of advice, but they are not the same. Confucius's proverb perhaps deserves the accolade "the Silver Rule": it is the principle of non-harm. The demand of the Golden Rule is greater: it is the principle of active service, even toward those who hate you. Here is the original context of Jesus' teaching. It is arguably the most sublime ethical teaching ever uttered (I admit I am biased):

If someone slaps you on one cheek, turn to them the other also. If someone takes your coat, do not withhold your shirt from them. Do to others as you would have them do to you. But, love your enemies, do good to them, and lend to them without expecting to get anything back. Then your reward will be great, and you will be children of the Most High, because he is kind to the ungrateful and wicked. Be merciful, just as your Father is merciful. (Luke 6:29–36)

The difference between the Silver Rule and the Golden Rule is significant. It is the difference between *choosing not to punch my enemy in the nose* and *deciding to build my enemy a hospital.*

But what of Hugh Mackay's suggestion that Jesus did not teach people to believe in doctrines, only to treat each other well? It seems to me that throughout Jesus' parables and the famous Sermon on the Mount he nearly always premises his statements on the "doctrines" of God's love and mercy. Because the Creator of the universe is loving and merciful, all of his creatures should reflect reality in the way they treat one another.

What we think lies at the heart of reality inevitably shapes what we think is an authentic human life. For example, if, like the famous atheist Friedrich Nietzsche, we believe that "survival of the fittest" is the heart of nature's reality, then (just like Nietzsche) we are going to view turning the other cheek and helping enemies in need as neither logically nor morally required. If, on the other hand, we think that God's love and mercy are the heartbeat of the universe, then suddenly everything in Jesus' famous Sermon on the Mount becomes both logically compelling and life enhancing.

This is precisely how Jesus framed his message in the famous passage quoted above. Why does it make sense to love our enemies? Because God himself is "kind to the ungrateful and wicked." Why would we be merciful, even to those who don't deserve it? Because, as Jesus put it, "your Father is merciful." We could almost say that Jesus never taught people how to treat each other without also telling them what to believe about God.

## REFLECTIONS

### Mere Tradition

Part of the challenge of being a follower of Christ today is regularly pausing to separate out mere "tradition" from the will of God revealed by the Teacher. Speaking personally, sometimes the process can be fun, as I realise that some of the things I have burdened myself with are just church culture. Other times it can be disturbing as it dawns on me that some of what counts as "normal" (in church or wider society) would be anathema to Jesus.

Following the Teacher will occasionally run counter to the world around us. It will at times be unpopular—a minority position. As Jesus warned in his Sermon on the Mount:

> Enter through the narrow gate. For wide is the gate and broad is the road that leads to destruction, and many enter through it. But small is the gate and narrow the road that leads to life, and only a few find it. (Matthew 7:13–14)

Jesus probably intended this as a specific description of the response of first-century Israel to his teaching. But it has been disturbingly true of other periods as well. Sometimes—though not always—following Christ as teacher is a lonely, countercultural experience. The wider public might like the idea of Jesus as teacher, but I am not sure it always has time for the actual content of his teaching. Some of what he said almost certainly puts aspects of Western culture (and church life) on the "broad road" rather than the "narrow" one.

## Culture and Christ

Christians have often said that applying Jesus' teaching to everyday life at times feels like driving the wrong way up a one-way street (to extend Jesus' road metaphor). But this is to be expected if Jesus' claims are true and he really is the divinely appointed Teacher.

A truth that is relevant for all human cultures will, by definition, contradict any particular human culture at some point, since societies are constantly in flux, sometimes coinciding with the truth, other times deviating from it.

People who seek to adjust Jesus' teaching—as the modern church sometimes does—in an attempt to make it more "relevant" often end up doing just the opposite. In the first century as much as the twenty-first, the power and poignancy of Jesus' teaching is that it sounds like a voice from outside human society. It is a voice that knows us only too well, and it calls on us to live beyond the historical blip of our particular culture.

## Being a Disciple

The counterpart to the theme of Jesus as a teacher is that the Christian is a *disciple*. The word "disciple," *mathētēs* in the original Greek of the Gospels, is the default term for a follower of Jesus—not just the so-called twelve apostles but *all* of his followers. It is used over two-hundred times. No other New Testament word for "Christian" is used anywhere near this often. "Disciple" translates literally as *learner* or *pupil*. It is the normal Greek word for a student in a school. It is, as I said, the counterpart to Christ's role as teacher.

The word "disciple" reminds us that the historical Jesus wanted not just "believers" who would pray and go to church but "students" who would imbibe his words and seek to relate them to everyday life. If the selection of teachings quoted at the end of this chapter is anything to go by, I think we can safely conclude that the historical Jesus would want to ask modern disciples a series of uncomfortable questions: Do you reflect on what I said about marriage and sex and allow that to shape how you think and act in our sexually loaded society? Do you mull over what I said about clothes, food, and the body (the obsessions of a pagan culture) and try to apply this to modern living? Do you ponder my teaching on poverty and wealth and factor that into your household budget? Do you recall how I urged you to pray and make that part of your routine? Do you contemplate my sayings on divine forgiveness and soak them up for yourself and embody them toward others? Have you learnt what I meant by "love your neighbour as yourself" and tried to express that in all of the radical ways I described?

## An Authentic Human Life

I once sat behind a car with a bumper sticker that read: *Be yourself. Nobody is better qualified.* That is what "authenticity" has come to mean today: being true to yourself. Speaking personally, that would be a very low bar! I am not sure I want to settle for my*self*, with all my foibles and blind spots. I want to be *more* than myself. I don't want to shape reality around who I am. I want to know what reality is and then allow that to shape me.

I can't help feeling that true authenticity (from the Greek word *authentikos,* meaning "genuine") is not about giving free expression to the subjective blip of my culture or personality. True authenticity would be about allowing our lives to be animated by what is objectively true in the universe. And *this* is what seems to be going on in the teaching of Jesus. A particular view of what is real—about the world, about God, and about his kingdom—shapes what it means to experience an authentic human life. The love of God, Jesus taught, inspires us to pursue love amidst the complexities of everyday life.

## A SELECTION OF READINGS FROM THE TEACHING OF JESUS

### Christian Character

Blessed are the poor in spirit, for theirs is the kingdom of heaven. Blessed are those who mourn, for they will be comforted. Blessed are the meek, for they will inherit the earth. Blessed are those who hunger and thirst for righteousness, for they will be filled. Blessed are the merciful, for they will be shown mercy. Blessed are the pure in heart, for they will see God. Blessed are the peacemakers, for they will be called children of God. Blessed are those who are persecuted because of righteousness, for theirs is the kingdom of heaven. (Matthew 5:3–10)

### Sex and Marriage

You have heard that it was said, "You shall not commit adultery." But I tell you that anyone who looks at a woman lustfully has already committed adultery with her in his heart. If your right eye causes you to stumble, gouge it out and throw it away. It is better for you to lose one part of your body than for your whole body to be thrown into hell. And if your right hand causes you to stumble, cut it off and throw it away. It is better for you to lose one part of your body than for your whole body to go into hell. (Matthew 5:27–30)

### How to Pray

And when you pray, do not be like the hypocrites, for they love to pray standing in the synagogues and on the street corners to be seen by others. Truly I tell you, they have received their reward in full. But when you pray, go into your room, close the door and pray to your Father, who is unseen. Then your Father, who sees what is done in secret, will reward you. And when you pray, do not keep on babbling like pagans, for they think they will be heard because of their many words. Do not be like them, for your Father knows what you need before you ask him. This, then, is how you should pray: "Our Father in heaven, hallowed be your name, your kingdom come, your will be done, on earth as it is in heaven. Give us today our daily bread. And forgive us our debts, as we also have forgiven our debtors. And lead us not into temptation, but deliver us from the evil one." (Matthew 6:5–13)

## Wealth, Food, and the Body

No one can serve two masters. Either you will hate the one and love the other, or you will be devoted to the one and despise the other. You cannot serve both God and money. Therefore I tell you, do not worry about your life, what you will eat or drink; or about your body, what you will wear. Is not life more than food, and the body more than clothes? Look at the birds of the air; they do not sow or reap or store away in barns, and yet your heavenly Father feeds them. Are you not much more valuable than they? Can any one of you by worrying add a single hour to your life? And why do you worry about clothes? See how the flowers of the field grow. They do not labor or spin. Yet I tell you that not even Solomon in all his splendor was dressed like one of these. If that is how God clothes the grass of the field, which is here today and tomorrow is thrown into the fire, will he not much more clothe you—you of little faith? So do not worry, saying, "What shall we eat?" or

"What shall we drink?" or "What shall we wear?" For the pagans run after all these things, and your heavenly Father knows that you need them. But seek first his kingdom and his righteousness, and all these things will be given to you as well. Therefore do not worry about tomorrow, for tomorrow will worry about itself. Each day has enough trouble of its own. (Matthew 6:24–34)

## Caring for Those in Need

On one occasion an expert in the law stood up to test Jesus. "Teacher," he asked, "what must I do to inherit eternal life?" "What is written in the Law?" he replied. "How do you read it?" He answered, "'Love the Lord your God with all your heart and with all your soul and with all your strength and with all your mind'; and, 'Love your neighbor as yourself.'" "You have answered correctly," Jesus replied. "Do this and you will live." But he wanted to justify himself, so he asked Jesus, "And who is my neighbor?" In reply Jesus said: "A man was going down from Jerusalem to Jericho, when he was attacked by robbers. They stripped him of his clothes, beat him and went away, leaving him half dead. A priest happened to be going down the same road, and when he saw the man, he passed by on the other side. So too, a Levite, when he came to the place and saw him, passed by on the other side. But a Samaritan, as he traveled, came where the man was; and when he saw him, he took pity on him. He went to him and bandaged his wounds, pouring on oil and wine. Then he put the man on his own donkey, brought him to an inn and took care of him. The next day he took out two denarii and gave them to the innkeeper. 'Look after him,' he said, 'and when I return, I will reimburse you for any extra expense you may have.'

Which of these three do you think was a neighbor to the man who fell into the hands of robbers?" The expert in the law replied, "The one who had mercy on him." Jesus told him, "Go and do likewise." (Luke 10:25–37)

## Love for Enemies

But to you who are listening I say: Love your enemies, do good to those who hate you, bless those who curse you, pray for those who mistreat you. If someone slaps you on one cheek, turn to them the other also. If someone takes your coat, do not withhold your shirt from them. Give to everyone who asks you, and if anyone takes what belongs to you, do not demand it back. Do to others as you would have them do to you. If you love those who love you, what credit is that to you? Even sinners love those who love them. And if you do good to those who are good to you, what credit is that to you? Even sinners do that. And if you lend to those from whom you expect repayment, what credit is that to you? Even sinners lend to sinners, expecting to be repaid in full. But love your enemies, do good to them, and lend to them without expecting to get anything back. Then your reward will be great, and you will be children of the Most High, because he is kind to the ungrateful and wicked. Be merciful, just as your Father is merciful. (Luke 6:27–36)

## Divine Mercy

Suppose one of you has a hundred sheep and loses one of them. Doesn't he leave the ninety-nine in the open country and go after the lost sheep until he finds it? And when he finds it, he joyfully puts it on his shoulders and goes home. Then he calls his friends and neighbors together and says, "Rejoice with me; I have found my lost sheep." I tell you that in the same way there will be more rejoicing in heaven over one sinner who repents than over ninety-nine righteous persons who do not need to repent. Or suppose a woman has ten silver coins and loses one. Doesn't she light a lamp, sweep the house and search carefully until she finds it? And when she finds it, she calls her friends and neighbors together and says, "Rejoice with me; I have found my lost coin." In the same way, I tell you, there is rejoicing in the presence of the angels of God over one sinner who repents. (Luke 15:4–10)

# 4

## HEALER:

### THE DEEDS THAT BAFFLE

We arrive at an aspect of Jesus' ministry that is simultaneously unavoidable and (for many) awkward. In our scientifically informed culture, talk of the blind receiving sight, the dead being raised, and storms being calmed seems like the baggage of an ignorant, superstitious past. Jesus the *teacher* we can appreciate, but Jesus the healer, miracle worker— that is a little less digestible. Nevertheless, no historical treatment of Christ can sidestep this major aspect of the early portraits of the man.

In this chapter I do not intend, or even believe it is possible, to prove that Jesus performed miracles. What I want to do is offer some philosophical and historical observations about miracles before turning to explore what the Gospels say is the meaning of Jesus' supposed startling deeds.

## PHILOSOPHICAL OBSERVATIONS ABOUT MIRACLES

The modern philosophical debate about miracles, which has been going on since the eighteenth century, has resulted in a stalemate—not a draw or friendly handshake, but a begrudging realisation that neither side has been able to deal the decisive blow.

Philosophically, the rationality (or otherwise) of a belief in miracles boils down to our background assumptions about the world we live in. If I assume that the laws of nature define what is possible in the universe, then the fact that I don't observe miracles today will be interpreted quite reasonably as proof that miracles have never been observed—indeed, could never occur. No amount of evidence will be considered strong enough to convince me of the "supernatural" nature of an event. I will always opt for a natural explanation, no matter how complex the explanation has to be. My assumption demands it.

On the other hand, if I believe that the observable laws of nature do not define the limits of what is possible in the universe—that there is a Law-giver behind and above these laws—then the fact that I personally do not observe miracles today will not be regarded as proof miracles have never occurred. It may inspire a certain skepticism about miraculous claims, but my assumption about a Law-giver (God) gives me the freedom to accept a "miraculous" interpretation of an event if the evidence points strongly enough in that direction.

## HISTORY NOTE

The great Scottish philosopher David Hume (1711–76) argued that no evidence should ever be considered strong enough to suggest that a miraculous event has occurred. Only if it is impossible to disbelieve a report about a miracle, he said, should a miracle be accepted, because then the falsehood of the report would be even more miraculous than the reported miracle itself. Hume's logic is well known but, as many have pointed out, his rule of evidence is entirely arbitrary and premised on the unstated assumption that miracles don't happen. It is a dictum designed to rule out miracles, not to probe if they are possible. Whether miracles are possible is not a matter of mere report or testimony but of the prior philosophical question of whether there is a God behind the laws of nature who is able to act powerfully within nature in ways that surprise us. If one has resolved that question (on other grounds) in favour of God's existence, then the only evidence a miracle would leave behind, short of experiencing a miracle for oneself, is the testimony or report of others. We may be entitled to be suspicious about such reports, but there is no sound reason to demand that such reports be impossible to reject before we accept them.

Put simply, openness to miracles is irrational if I assume there is no God and it is rational if I hold that there is a God. Hence, the debate about miracles often moves on to a debate over *naturalism* (the affirmation that physical forces are the only forces in the universe) versus *theism* (the affirmation that a Creative Mind stands behind the order of the universe). In philosophy there is something of a stalemate there, too. This is not the book to unravel these mysteries. I simply want to underline that belief in miracles is not really a historical question; it is a philosophical one.

Turning from philosophy to history, let me make a few brief observations.

## The Absence of Miracle Workers in Jesus' World

It is sometimes said that miracle workers were commonplace in Jesus' day and that the Gospels should be read in light of that wider trend in the ancient world. Everyone was doing miracles, so the Gospel writers portrayed Jesus as doing the same! This is not quite true.

While Jewish exorcists (those who cast out demons) appear to have been common, there are only two Jewish historical figures other than Jesus associated with healing miracles in this period. The first is Honi the Circledrawer who, in the century before Jesus, is reported to have prayed to God for rain during a drought. He stood inside a circle drawn on the ground and waited until God answered the prayer, which he reportedly did. The story is mentioned 150 years after the fact by the historian Josephus (*Jewish Antiquities* 14.22–24), and another century after that in the Mishnah (Ta'anit 3:8).

The second figure is Hanina ben Dosa who lived in Galilee a generation after Jesus. According to a source written a few centuries later, Hanina prayed for the desperately ill son of the famous Jerusalem rabbi, Gamaliel, and the boy dramatically recovered (Talmud Berakhot 34b).

From the historical perspective, it is difficult to know what to conclude about such isolated stories recorded a hundred or more years after the event in one or two sources. My point, however, is that even if these are real historical remembrances (and I lean toward that conclusion), the parallel with Jesus is minimal if not nonexistent. Honi and Hanina were not really miracle workers. They were pious Jews with a reputation for having their prayers answered.

What we have in the Gospels is another thing entirely. Not only is the sheer number of Jesus' reported miracles striking (thirty-eight by scholarly count), so is the fact that they are said to occur through his own power. He restores a leper with a touch, a crippled man with a word, a dead girl with a command, a hemorrhaging woman by her contact with his robe, a demon-crazed man with a simple rebuke, and so on.

Another figure is sometimes put forward as a promising comparison to Jesus as a direct miracle-worker. It comes from the "pagan," or Graeco-Roman, side of the ancient world. Apollonius of Tyanna wandered the Mediterranean as a philosopher and holy man until his death sometime before the year AD 100. He left no documentation or even disciples, but a biography was written about him 120 years later by the philosopher Philostratus (AD 172–250). Throughout the biography Apollonius is said to have healed the sick, given sight to the blind, and even raised the dead. Scholars often note that some of the stories are curiously similar to accounts about Jesus. This may not be an accident. By the time Philostratus wrote his biography of Apollonius, the New Testament Gospels had become hugely popular, and many people in the region were embracing the Christian faith. Many scholars think that Philostratus probably wrote his *Life of Apollonius* to provide the Greek public with a pagan parallel to Jesus. "It is pure hagiography," writes Oxford University's Michael Frede, "and has parallels with the life of Jesus that are so obvious as to be considered intentional" (Michael Frede. "Apollonius [14] of Tyana." *Brill's New Pauly.* http://referenceworks.brillonlinc.com/browse/brill-s-new-pauly). Whatever the motives behind the biography, everything we learn about Apollonius's miracle-working activity comes from this one source written well over a century after the man's death. The contrast with the data concerning Jesus is striking, as the next section explains.

## Jesus' Healings in the Historical Sources

The startling deeds of Jesus are attested in multiple independent sources in both Christian and non-Christian writings. On the Christian side, Mark, Q, L, M, SQ, Paul, and James all provide evidence of Jesus' healing abilities. To repeat what I said in chapter 1, these "Christian" sources are treated by historians as independent witnesses since, although they now appear together in our New Testament, they were originally separate traditions. Something other than collusion, in other words, gave rise to the consistent portrayal of Jesus as a miracle worker.

From the Jewish and Graeco-Roman sources we have at least two references to Jesus' miraculous activity. The first-century Jewish historian Josephus wrote: "At this time there appeared Jesus, a wise man. For he was a doer of startling deeds . . ."(*Jewish Antiquities* 18.63) The word translated "startling" here is the Greek term *paradoxos*, from which we get "paradox." It is a neutral, non-committal way of referring to Christ's inexplicable abilities.

Not so neutral is the legal judgment of the Jewish Talmud: "On the eve of Passover Jesus was hanged (i.e., on a cross) . . . because he has practised sorcery and enticed and led Israel astray." (bar. Sanhedrin 43a). What is fascinating is that amongst Jesus' opponents there was never any attempt to deny Jesus' strange abilities, only to cast them in a negative light, as involving "sorcery" or the power of demons.

## What Modern Historians Say About Jesus' Miracles

It is because Jesus'"startling deeds" are so widely and independently attested in ancient writings that most modern experts (whatever their religious persuasion) arrive at a similar conclusion: Jesus did things that were interpreted by everyone around him as supernatural. My precise wording is intentional. Historians cannot affirm (or deny) that Jesus actually did miracles. That would go beyond historical method to philosophical interpretation. What historians can (and do) affirm is that Jesus' friends and foes alike all conceded the supernatural nature of his ministry. This is a conclusion reached by virtually every scholar working in the field across the world.

Someone who has written more than most on the topic is prolific historical Jesus scholar John P. Meier of the University of Notre Dame in the United States. His *magnum opus* is the (so far) five-volume *A Marginal Jew: Rethinking the Historical Jesus* published slowly between 1991 and 2016. Five hundred pages of volume 2 are given over to a rather exacting analysis of the historical data concerning Jesus' miracles. Meier happily rejects all sorts of details within the Gospels—he is no apologist—but his conclusion about the basic fact of Jesus' reputation to heal people is strong:

> The miracle traditions about Jesus' public ministry are already so widely attested in various sources and literary forms by the end of the first Christian generation that total fabrication by the early church is, practically speaking, impossible. . . . Put dramatically but with not too much exaggeration: if the miracle tradition from Jesus' public ministry were to be rejected in toto as unhistorical, so should every other Gospel

tradition about him. For if the criteria of historicity do not work in the case of the miracle tradition, where multiple attestation is so massive and coherence so impressive, there is no reason to expect them to work elsewhere. The quest would simply have to be abandoned. Needless to say, that is not the conclusion we have reached here. (John P. Meier, *A Marginal Jew: Rethinking the Historical Jesus*. 5 vols. New York: Doubleday, 1994, 2:630–31.)

That is where historical analysis of the question of Jesus' miracles leads us. That is also where it leaves us. How we go on from here to interpret this historical conclusion involves, as I have said, our prior assumptions. If we assume that the observable laws of nature define the parameters of what can happen in the universe, then we will feel well justified in searching for a natural interpretation of the data. If, on the other hand, we hold that there is a Law-giver behind the laws of nature who can work powerfully within nature, then, given the direction in which the historical evidence points, we will feel well justified in accepting a metaphysical interpretation of the evidence and conclude with the Gospels that Jesus really did perform "startling deeds." What this conclusion actually means, according to the Gospels, is our next topic.

**BOOK NOTES** | Perhaps the most rigorous analysis of philosophical and historical issues relating to Jesus' miracles is the two-volume study by Craig Keener, *Miracles: The Credibility of New Testament Accounts*. Vol.1–2. Grand Rapids: Baker, 2011. Keener displays extraordinary breadth of learning, in both history and philosophy, and he does what no other writer (I've seen) has attempted before: he brings in a wealth of recent documentation about modern unexplained healings, verified through medical records and compelling witness reports. This combination of historical, philosophical, and contemporary studies of miracles makes this a unique resource for anyone interested in exploring the topic at the highest intellectual level.

## UNDOING ISRAEL'S CURSE

Throughout this book I don't intend to expound the Gospel texts. I simply want to give readers some tools for reading the Gospels in a plausible historical framework. I think of it as a kind of *CliffsNotes* for Jesus (although I hope readers will study the set texts as well!).

What, then, is the significance of Jesus' miracles from the point of view of the first-century Gospels? In addition to displaying Christ's power and compassion, the miracles have at least two important dimensions. The first has to do with ancient Israel specifically; the second has to do with the entire creation.

At the heart of the Jewish faith (the faith which Jesus shared) was a "covenant," or agreement, between God and Israel made 1,300 years before Christ. God promised to bless Israel as long as the nation reciprocated with worship of the Creator and justice toward other creatures. If Israel refused the path of worship and justice, the nation would experience a host of agreed-upon, nationwide disasters. In the fifth book of the Old Testament (what Jews call the Tanak) Moses outlined some of the unhappy outcomes:

> However, if you do not obey the LORD your God and do not carefully follow all his commands and decrees I am giving you today, all these curses will come upon you and overtake you . . . The LORD will strike you with wasting disease, with fever and inflammation . . . The LORD will cause you to be defeated before your enemies . . . The LORD will afflict you with the boils of Egypt and with tumors, festering sores and the itch, from which you cannot be cured. The LORD will afflict you with madness, blindness and confusion of mind. (Deuteronomy 28:15–28)

Many Jews in Jesus' day believed themselves to be living under precisely these covenant curses, and justifiably so. According to the Old Testament, between the ninth and sixth centuries BC Israel did turn its back on its agreement with God. The nation courted pagan deities and mistreated the poor and the marginalised. As a result (so the Jewish people affirmed), God let his chosen people be conquered by invaders, beginning with the Assyrians in the eighth century BC, the Babylonians in sixth century BC, the Greeks in the fourth–third centuries BC, and climaxing with the Romans in the first century BC. Israel's God also allowed the nation to be plagued with all manner of diseases: fever, leprosy, blindness, and demon-crazed madness. The covenant curses had fallen upon them.

The only thing mitigating Jewish despondency in this period was the presence in the same Scriptures of prophecies stating that, after a period of judgment, Israel would again experience a time of healing and restoration. The prophet Isaiah seven hundred years before Christ declared:

> Then will the eyes of the blind be opened
>> and the ears of the deaf unstopped.
> Then will the lame leap like a deer,
>> and the mute tongue shout for joy.
>
> (Isaiah 35:5–6)

Later in the same book the prophet says this healing would come about through the ministry of a mysterious "Servant of the Lord." The Servant would himself bear the punishment of Israel and so deliver his people from the covenant curses:

> Surely he took up our pain
>> and bore our suffering,
> yet we considered him punished by God,
>> stricken by him, and afflicted.
> But he was pierced for our transgressions,
>> he was crushed for our iniquities;
> the punishment that brought us peace was on him,
>> and by his wounds we are healed.
>
> (Isaiah 53:4–5)

It is precisely in this biblical context that the healings of Jesus can, in large part, be understood. Jesus repeatedly healed just the sorts of ailments mentioned in the Old Testament (fever, skin disease, blindness, madness, lameness, and so on). This was a sign to ancient Jews that the covenant curses were being *lifted* from Israel. This is exactly how the Gospel of Matthew interprets Jesus' ministry. At the end of his account of the healing of a leper and a lame man Matthew writes:

> When Jesus came into Peter's house, he saw Peter's mother-in-law lying in bed with a fever. He touched her hand and the fever left her, and she got up and began to wait on him. When evening came, many who were demon-possessed were brought to him, and he drove out the spirits with a word and healed all the sick. This was to fulfill what was spoken through the prophet Isaiah [in the passage quoted above]: "He took up our infirmities and bore our diseases." (Matthew 8:14–17)

Three chapters later, Jesus explains his miracles in terms of the promises of Isaiah 35 quoted earlier:

> When John [the Baptist], who was in prison, heard about the deeds of the Messiah, he sent his disciples to ask him, "Are you the one who is to come, or should we expect someone else?" Jesus replied, "Go back and report to John what you hear and see: The blind receive sight, the lame walk, those who have leprosy are cleansed, the deaf hear, the dead are raised, and the good news is proclaimed to the poor [phrases all taken from the prophet Isaiah, quoted earlier]." (Matthew 11:2–5)

In short, Jesus' healing ministry constituted a profound theological statement to Israel that the covenant curses described in the Old Testament book of Deuteronomy and elsewhere were being lifted in the ministry of Christ. The old covenant, with its blessings and curses, was being annulled; God's new covenant (for all nations) was being enacted.

## A FORETASTE OF GOD'S KINGDOM

There is a second, equally important, biblical understanding of the miracles of Jesus. Put simply, Jesus' deeds are portrayed in our texts as a sign within history of the restoration of all things at the end of history. Jesus' power over sickness, evil, and nature are a preview, you might say, of God's coming kingdom. This is a point Jesus himself makes at the end of a dispute with the Pharisees (a strict sect of first-century Jews) in the Gospel of Matthew:

> Then they brought him a demon-possessed man who was blind and mute, and Jesus healed him, so that he could both talk and see. All the people were astonished and said, "Could this be the Son of David?" But when the Pharisees heard this, they said, "It is only by Beelzebul, the prince of demons, that this fellow drives out demons." Jesus knew their thoughts and said to them, "Every kingdom divided against itself will be ruined, and every city or household divided against itself will not stand. If Satan drives out Satan, he is divided against himself. How then can his kingdom stand? And if I drive out demons by Beelzebul, by whom do your people drive them out? So then, they will be your judges. But if it is by the Spirit

of God that I drive out demons, then the kingdom of God
has come upon you." (Matthew 12:22–28)

For the Pharisees, Jesus' miracles indicated the presence of
devilish sorcery ("Beelzebul" is a term for "the devil"). The same
point is reiterated in the Jewish text discussed earlier (Jesus "practised sorcery"). For Jesus, though, his healing work indicates the
presence not of the "prince of demons" but of God's kingdom. He
insists, "But if it is by the Spirit of God that I drive out demons,
then the kingdom of God has come upon you" (Matthew 12:28).

Usually, the "kingdom of God" is described as a future reality.
It refers to the moment when all creation will be brought into
conformity with the wise and loving purposes of the Creator. The
technical word for this is *eschatology*. Justice will reign, peace will
ensue, and all nature will thrive and flourish. In the well-known
Lord's Prayer (or "Our Father"), for instance, Jesus taught his
disciples to pray "Your kingdom come," a plea for God's dominion
over the world to come soon. In the passage just quoted, though,
Jesus describes that kingdom as present in some way in his ministry
of healing and exorcism: "the kingdom of God has come upon you,"
he says. What was usually described by Jesus (and other biblical
writers) as an ultimate *future* reality is glimpsed, he reckoned,
in his startling deeds. The renowned classicist and historian of
religion David Flusser (a Jew not a Christian) puts the point well
in his study of Jesus' life:

> [Jesus] established his claim to the eschatological office by
> pointing to his preaching of salvation and to his supernatural
> works of healing. Jesus saw these things as an unmistakable

sign that the era of salvation had already dawned. (Flusser, *The Sage of Galilee: Rediscovering Jesus' Genius*, 28.)

According to Christian Scripture, only in the final kingdom of God will there be no more pain, death, and discord. As the second-to-last chapter of the New Testament envisions:

He [God] will wipe every tear from their eyes. There will be no more death or mourning or crying or pain, for the old order of things has passed away. (Revelation 21:4)

What is promised in prophecy and vision here in the book of Revelation (and elsewhere) was, the Gospels say, temporarily experienced within history in the ministry of Jesus. Evil was overthrown, frail bodies were restored, and nature itself was put right. The "kingdom of God" had *in miniature* come upon them. And, as we have seen, it left its mark throughout the ancient sources. As much as the miracles point to Jesus' compassion and authority, more fundamentally they preview the renewal of all things in the kingdom to which Jesus invited his hearers.

# REFLECTIONS

## Miracles Today?

For Christian believers in my readership I should probably add that I do believe that God in his mercy chooses to heal people today—sometimes through prayers, sometimes without them. He did this in Old Testament times; he will do it in contemporary times, the New Testament assures us (e.g., James 5:14–16). In my view, the many fully verified unexplained medical recoveries are the "miraculous" work of the Creator, whether or not the people involved are Christians, or prayed.

But I want to stress this is not what the Gospels are trying to teach us in their accounts of Jesus' miracles (nor is it a point I wish to stress in a book like this). What Jesus did within history was not a program that is meant to be enacted in the ongoing life of the church; it is rather a window into a future kingdom that is hoped for and proclaimed by the church.

## Restless Hope

The purpose of Jesus' startling deeds was not to evoke a belief in miracles today but rather to inspire a longing for the day when God's kingdom comes fully upon the world. That's the perspective of the Gospels. Throughout history, Christian faith has always involved a restless hope—a hope captured perfectly in the prayer "Your kingdom come"! The previews of the kingdom glimpsed in Jesus' miracles have typically made Christ's followers dissatisfied with the way things are and desperate for the way things Christ said they would one day be. Christian hope is thus confident but restless: it praises God for the preview (in Jesus' life) and pleads him for the finale (in the "kingdom come"), when evil will be overthrown, humanity healed, and creation itself renewed.

## A Program for Church and Society

Throughout the ages this restless hope has also inspired diligent work while waiting. Christians pray not only "Your kingdom come" but also "Your will be done on earth as it is in heaven." In theory— and others can judge if this is worked out in practice—people who have glimpsed the future in the healing deeds of Jesus commit themselves to serving the world, just as he did, in whatever way they can this side of the kingdom. They relieve suffering at every opportunity and resist evil wherever they see it. The creation of Christian hospitals and hospices in fourth-century AD Rome and the (largely Christian) movement to abolish slavery in eighteenth-century England were, in part, motivated by this ancient (theo)logic.

Recently I was in Rome shooting scenes for a documentary (on this mixed history of the church) about a remarkable woman who, while virtually unknown today, was amongst the most notable women of the fourth century. Fabiola was born into one of the founding families of Rome and was one of the capital's wealthiest people. She suffered greatly in an abusive marriage before gaining rare permission to divorce her husband and begin again. At some point she met Christians, who by this period could be found in all ranks of imperial society. She heard the news about Christ and devoted herself to the powerful, tender Master we read about in the Gospels. What Fabiola did next was extraordinary. She sold her entire holdings, turned it into cash, and devoted herself, and all her resources, to assisting the poor and sick of Rome. She established what may well have been the first public hospital in history. Hospitals were part of the military apparatus of the empire, of course, but the idea of throwing open the doors of medical care to the whole population was novel. Remarkably, she tended to people not just with her money but with her own hands. "How often she carried on her own shoulders poor filthy wretches tortured by epilepsy!" wrote an eyewitness and friend. "How often did she wash away the purulent [pus-like] matter from wounds which others could not even endure to look at! She gave food with her own hand, and even when a man was but a breathing corpse, she would moisten his lips with drops of water." She expanded her operation. "Rome was not large enough for her kindness. She went from island to island, and travelled round the Etruscan Sea, bestowing her bounty" (Jerome, *Letters*. Translated by F. A. Wright. Loeb Classical Library 262. Cambridge, MA: Harvard University Press, 1933, 77.6).

In *this* sense Jesus' healing ministry recorded in the Gospels *did* provide a program for the church in society—not in the ministry of "faith healers" but in practical attempts to repair what is broken in the world. The logic is simple: we might not yet possess all the resources of the "kingdom come" but we do know its aims—to renew human life and put an end to evil—and these aims shape what we strive for here and now. That is the theory. I am painfully aware the church hasn't always lived up to its confession of Jesus the Healer.

## A SELECTION OF READINGS FROM JESUS' STARTLING DEEDS

### Healing of a Disabled Man

A few days later, when Jesus again entered Capernaum, the people heard that he had come home. They gathered in such large numbers that there was no room left, not even outside the door, and he preached the word to them. Some men came, bringing to him a paralyzed man, carried by four of them. Since they could not get him to Jesus because of the crowd, they made an opening in the roof above Jesus by digging through it and then lowered the mat the man was lying on. When Jesus saw their faith, he said to the paralyzed man, "Son, your sins are forgiven." Now some teachers of the law were sitting there, thinking to themselves, "Why does this fellow talk like that? He's blaspheming! Who can forgive sins but God alone?" Immediately Jesus knew in his spirit that this was what they were thinking in their hearts, and he said to them, "Why are you thinking these things? Which is easier: to say to this paralyzed man, 'Your sins are forgiven,' or to say, 'Get up, take your mat and walk'? But I want you to know that the Son of Man has authority on earth to forgive sins." So he said to the man, "I tell you, get up, take your mat and go home." He got up, took his mat and walked out in full view of them all. This amazed everyone and they praised God, saying, "We have never seen anything like this!" (Mark 2:1–12)

## Healing of a Leper and a Servant

When Jesus came down from the mountainside, large crowds followed him. A man with leprosy came and knelt before him and said, "Lord, if you are willing, you can make me clean." Jesus reached out his hand and touched the man. "I am willing," he said. "Be clean!" Immediately he was cleansed of his leprosy. Then Jesus said to him, "See that you don't tell anyone. But go, show yourself to the priest and offer the gift Moses commanded, as a testimony to them." When Jesus had entered Capernaum, a centurion came to him, asking for help. "Lord," he said, "my servant lies at home paralyzed, suffering terribly." Jesus said to him, "Shall I come and heal him?" The centurion replied, "Lord, I do not deserve to have you come under my roof. But just say the word, and my servant will be healed. For I myself am a man under authority, with soldiers under me. I tell this one, 'Go,' and he goes; and that one, 'Come,' and he comes. I say to my servant, 'Do this,' and he does it." When Jesus heard this, he was amazed and said to those following him, "Truly I tell you, I have not found anyone in Israel with such great faith. I say to you that many will come from the east and the west, and will take their places at the feast with Abraham, Isaac and Jacob in the kingdom of heaven. But the subjects of the kingdom will be thrown outside, into the darkness, where there will be weeping and gnashing of teeth." Then Jesus said to the centurion, "Go! Let it be done just as you believed it would." And his servant was healed at that moment. (Matthew 8:1–13)

## Turning Water into Wine

On the third day a wedding took place at Cana in Galilee. Jesus' mother was there, and Jesus and his disciples had also been invited to the wedding. When the wine was gone, Jesus' mother said to him, "They have no more wine." "Woman, why do you involve me?" Jesus replied. "My hour has not yet come." His mother said to the servants, "Do whatever he tells you." Nearby stood six stone water jars, the kind used by the Jews for ceremonial washing, each holding from twenty to thirty gallons. Jesus said to the servants, "Fill the jars with water"; so they filled them to the brim. Then he told them, "Now draw some out and take it to the master of the banquet." They did so, and the master of the banquet tasted the water that had been turned into wine. He did not realize where it had come from, though the servants who had drawn the water knew. Then he called the bridegroom aside and said, "Everyone brings out the choice wine first and then the cheaper wine after the guests have had too much to drink; but you have saved the best till now." What Jesus did here in Cana of Galilee was the first of the signs through which he revealed his glory; and his disciples believed in him. (John 2:1–11)

## Healing of a Bleeding Woman and Raising of a Dead Child

When Jesus had again crossed over by boat to the other side of the lake, a large crowd gathered around him while he was by the lake. Then one of the synagogue leaders, named Jairus, came, and when he saw Jesus, he fell at his feet. He pleaded earnestly with him, "My little daughter is dying. Please come and put your hands on her so that she will be healed and live." So Jesus went with him. A large crowd followed and pressed around him. And a woman was there who had been subject to bleeding for twelve years. She had suffered a great deal under the care of many doctors and had spent all she had, yet instead of getting better she grew worse. When she heard about Jesus, she came up behind him in the crowd and touched his cloak, because she thought, "If I just touch his clothes, I will be healed." Immediately her bleeding stopped and she felt in her body that she was freed from her suffering. At once Jesus realized that power had gone out from him. He turned around in the crowd and asked, "Who touched my clothes?" "You see the people crowding against you," his disciples answered, "and yet you can ask, 'Who touched me?'" But Jesus kept looking around to see who had done it. Then the woman, knowing what had happened to her, came and fell at his feet and, trembling with fear, told him the whole truth. He said to her, "Daughter, your faith has healed you. Go in peace and be freed from your suffering." While Jesus was still speaking, some people came from the house of Jairus, the synagogue leader. "Your daughter is dead," they said. "Why bother the teacher anymore?" Overhearing what they said, Jesus told him, "Don't be afraid; just believe." He did not let anyone follow him except Peter, James and John the brother of James. When they came to the home of the synagogue leader, Jesus saw a commotion, with people crying and wailing loudly. He went in and said to them, "Why all this commotion and wailing? The child is not dead but asleep." But they laughed at him. After he put them all out, he took the child's father and mother and the disciples who were with him, and went in where the child was. He took her by the hand and said to her, "*Talitha koum*!" (which means "Little girl, I say to you, get up!"). Immediately the girl stood up and began to walk around (she was twelve years old). At this they were completely astonished. He gave strict orders not to let anyone know about this, and told them to give her something to eat. (Mark 5:21–43)

# 5

## ISRAEL:
## A NATION ON HIS SHOULDERS

**H**ave you ever come in halfway through a conversation and completely misunderstood what people were talking about? Perhaps you arrived just as your wife was criticising her "good-for-nothing husband," only to realise a moment later she was actually describing Homer Simpson in an episode from the cartoon series. Or perhaps you wandered past a good friend as he was mouthing off about Aborigines and denigrating "so-called refugees," only to discover with some relief that he was actually recounting the unfortunate views of someone he just heard on radio.

Sometimes, studying the life of Christ is like dropping in halfway through a conversation. You read an account in the Gospels and you are not quite sure what it is all about. It seems there is some historical detail you are missing or some Old Testament background the Gospel writers expect you to know. Having this background illuminates the entire conversation and offers new insights into well-known but little understood aspects of Jesus' life or teaching.

I want to explore an important claim in the Gospels that

assumes we have all been in on the conversation for a while. That conversation started back in the Old Testament, the Scriptures of ancient Israel. Once this aspect of Christ's life is set within that centuries-old conversation, an obscure and often overlooked part of the Jesus narrative brims with significance, both historical and personal.

Before we turn to Christ himself let me bring readers up to speed on the "conversation" the Gospel writers simply assume we have been part of: *the biblical story of Israel.*

## A SPECTATOR'S GUIDE TO ANCIENT ISRAEL

Despite some occasional bad press, the Old Testament tells a very straightforward narrative about God and his chosen nation, Israel. The story could be compared to an action-romance with more than a hint of tragedy: a noble prince rescues a slave girl, falls in love with her and marries her, only to have his heart broken by her unfaithfulness. That is the basic plot of the Hebrew Scriptures. In fact, one of the Old Testament prophets uses a very similar analogy when recalling the history of God's people (see the reading from Ezekiel 16 at the end of this chapter).

The story of Israel begins somewhere around 2000–1800 BC when, according to Genesis, the first book of the Old Testament, the Creator chose an idol-worshipping Mesopotamian named Abraham to be the patriarch of a brand new nation, one that would be divinely blessed and which would bring blessings to all the nations. Within a few generations, Abraham's descendants had grown into a sizable collective of twelve family clans, or tribes. These tribes were the direct descendants of the twelve sons of Jacob, the grandson of Abraham. Jacob's other name was "Israel," which is why the twelve clans born to him came to be known collectively as Israel (from the Hebrew verb "to strive, contend"). The family tree can get confusing. Don't worry about the details.

Sadly for the chosen people, the next few hundred years were spent not in the land promised by God (the future "land of Israel") but in Egypt where, under the Pharaohs, they suffered the indignities of a slave nation set to work on the massive building programs of northern Egypt. God's people would not be oppressed for long, however. Under the leadership of Moses the Israelites found deliverance, an "exodus" from slavery. The second book of the Old Testament, which is called Exodus, describes a series of divine disasters inflicted upon the tyrannous Egyptians resulting in the Pharaoh's decision to release the Israelites from slavery. In an event celebrated to this day in the Jewish Passover festival, God rescued his people out of their distress and started them on their journey toward the promised land.

If the story so far can be likened to a prince rescuing his beloved, the next part of Israel's history reads like the marriage. A few months after the exodus from Egypt, God called Moses to go up a mountain somewhere in the Sinai Peninsula where he received an entire national constitution, known to Jews as torah or "instruction." These laws would guide the newly liberated people of God as they settled in the land of Israel—the famous Ten Commandments were part of this constitution. The account of these laws—God's "marriage contract" with Israel, we might say—fills the bulk of the next few biblical books (Exodus, Leviticus, Numbers, and Deuteronomy).

The publisher insists that I reference here my *Doubter's Guide to the Ten Commandments: How, for Better or Worse, Our Ideas about the Good Life Come from Moses and Jesus* (Grand Rapids: Zondervan, 2016). It explains the meaning of each of the commandments and describes their impact on the history of Western ethics.

**BOOK NOTES**

The marriage, however, got off to a shaky start. No sooner had the nation agreed to live by this divine charter than they began to betray their rescuer in a host of ways. Between exiting Egypt and entering the promised land the twelve tribes lived as nomads in the deserts south and east of their future home. This forty-year period in Israel's history is known as the wanderings—a description of both the geographical and moral realities of the time. There were some spectacular national "sins" during the desert wanderings, including making and worshipping a golden calf (Exodus 32:1–6), constant grumbling against God and Moses (Numbers 14:26–35), and a mass pagan orgy of Israelite men with Moabite women (Numbers 25:1–3). Many such incidents are retold in the brutally honest books of the Bible.

I wish I could say that God and Israel were soon reconciled and lived happily ever after. Instead, these desert wanderings contain in miniature the basic plot of the whole Old Testament narrative. While the twelve tribes of Israel do eventually enter the promised land (sometime in the 1200s BC) and set up a successful monarchy and military machine (around 1000 BC), the spiritual story told alongside this political account makes for depressing reading.

(The period from the entry to the promised land to the rise of a powerful monarchic state is recounted in the Old Testament books of Joshua, Judges, Ruth, and 1 and 2 Samuel.) Israel oppressed her poor, worshipped pagan deities, and, despite the efforts of the prophets (750 BC–600 BC), the nation refused to heed the call for reform. The Old Testament reaches its lowest point with Israel exiled from its own land at the hands of the invading Babylonians (586 BC), leaving us wondering whether the Almighty's patience has run out. (The tragic events of Israel's fall from divine favour are narrated in the Old Testament books of 1 and 2 Kings and 1 and 2 Chronicles.) The Old Testament prophets not only warned of destruction, they predicted a time of restoration for the twelve tribes of Israel, and not just for Israel but for the whole world. (The pleas and promises of Israel's prophets are contained in the Old Testament books of Isaiah, Jeremiah, Ezekiel, Hosea, and others.) This is where the New Testament picks up the story.

This potted history of biblical Israel sets the scene for the Gospels' portrait of Jesus. It is the first part of the conversation the Gospel writers invite us to join. To state things simply, but not inaccurately, the Gospels portray Jesus as the *new Israel*. In him the entire story of God's people is being reenacted, fulfilled, pardoned, and rewritten.

## JESUS AS ISRAEL CALLED OUT OF EGYPT

Matthew's Gospel highlights this theme as early as his second chapter. According to Matthew, Jesus' family avoided the wrath of King Herod by fleeing to Egypt—where there was a large Jewish community at the time. What is striking is that the infant Jesus' return from Egypt back to the land of Israel is described by Matthew as the fulfilment of an Old Testament statement specifically about how God had formerly rescued the nation of Israel from the land of Egypt. Here is the passage:

> So he [Joseph] got up, took the child and his mother during the night and left for Egypt, where he stayed until the death of Herod. And so was fulfilled what the Lord had said through the prophet: "Out of Egypt I called my son." . . . So [after Herod's death] he got up, took the child and his mother and went to the land of Israel. (Matthew 2:14–15, 21)

The prophetic words quoted by Matthew, "Out of Egypt I called my son," come from the Old Testament book of Hosea 11:1. Everyone in Matthew's readership knew that this statement originally referred to the liberation of Israel from Egyptian slavery centuries earlier. "When Israel was a child, I loved him," said the prophet on behalf of God, "and out of Egypt I called my son. But the more they were called, the more they went away from me" (Hosea 11:1–2).

Hosea, writing in the eighth century BC, is lamenting the fact that, although God had rescued Israel from Egyptian slavery, the nation repaid him by refusing to follow his ways. As we have seen, this happened pretty much straight away. No sooner had they received God's laws (torah) than they invented ways of breaking them during the forty years of desert wanderings.

Matthew takes Hosea's statement about ancient Israel, God's national son, and applies it to Jesus, God's actual son. Just like Israel, Matthew says, Jesus was "called out of Egypt" and led back to the promised land. Attentive first-century readers will have begun to scratch their heads trying to work out in what way Jesus might mirror ancient Israel. In particular, they will have wondered if this new "son" would, like ancient Israel, refuse to heed the call of the Father. A few chapters later Matthew provides an answer to that question.

## JESUS AS ISRAEL IN THE DESERT

One of the strangest incidents in Christ's life is recorded in different forms in three of the four Gospels (Matthew, Mark, and Luke). Matthew's and Luke's reports of the episode are very similar and, in the opinion of most scholars, their accounts derive from their earlier shared source (known as Q). According to the passage, before Jesus embarked on his public career as a teacher and healer, he underwent a gruelling forty-day wandering through the deserts of southern Israel.

At one level, a desert sojourn is not a surprising event. Other holy men of the period are known to have been active in the desert, including those who left us the famous Dead Sea Scrolls. What is striking is that Jesus chose to wander the wilderness for exactly forty days. More than that, the temptations he faced during this period bear an uncanny resemblance to those faced by Israel in the famous forty-year wanderings described in the Old Testament books of Exodus, Numbers, and Deuteronomy.

Keep in mind that the "temptations" described in the following passage are probably meant to be thought of as a *visionary* experience at the climax of Jesus' forty-day fast. I will quote the text from Matthew, then draw out some of the Old Testament connections:

Then Jesus was led by the Spirit into the wilderness to be tempted by the devil. After fasting for forty days and forty nights, he was hungry. The tempter came to him and said, "If you are the Son of God, tell these stones to become bread."

Jesus answered, "It is written: 'Man shall not live on bread alone, but on every word that comes from the mouth of God.'"

Then the devil took him to the holy city and had him stand on the highest point of the temple. "If you are the Son of God," he said, "throw yourself down. For it is written:

'He will command his angels concerning you,
and they will lift you up in their hands,
so that you will not strike your foot against a stone.'"

Jesus answered him, "It is also written: 'Do not put the Lord your God to the test.'"

Again, the devil took him to a very high mountain and showed him all the kingdoms of the world and their splendor. "All this I will give you," he said, "if you will bow down and worship me."

Jesus said to him, "Away from me, Satan! For it is written: 'Worship the Lord your God, and serve him only.'"

Then the devil left him, and angels came and attended him. (Matthew 4:1–11)

If we were not aware of the story of Israel described earlier, we might have glanced over this scene and missed its great significance for the Gospels' conversation about Jesus.

Jesus' forty-day desert trial appears to recall, indeed reenact, Israel's forty-year desert trial a millennium or so before. The comparison is clear not just from the number forty and the desert location, but especially from the fact that the temptations Jesus faced during this time are precisely those Israel faced during its wanderings. And all of the biblical quotations Jesus threw back at the devil come straight out of the Old Testament account of Israel's forty years in the desert. To anyone well versed in the ongoing conversation of Israel, Matthew 4 provides a powerful picture of someone reenacting Israel's past and, by succeeding where Israel failed, rewriting the future. The details are intriguing, so I will unpack them.

The first of Israel's three great temptations in the desert concerned food. The wandering nation grew sick and tired of eating "manna from heaven" (divinely provided sustenance). They complained to Moses and arrogantly demanded that he arrange something more interesting for them: surely, if God could bend the might of Egypt, he could serve up a decent meal or two! Moses rebuked them for their ungrateful grumbling in words recorded in the Old Testament book of Deuteronomy:

> Remember how the LORD your God led you all the way in the wilderness these forty years, to humble and test you in order to know what was in your heart, whether or not you would keep his commands. He humbled you, causing you to hunger and then feeding you with manna, which neither you nor your ancestors had known, to teach you that man does not live on bread alone but on every word that comes from the mouth of the LORD. (Deuteronomy 8:2–3)

Notice that the closing words, "man does not live on bread alone . . . ," are exactly the words Jesus quotes when tempted to turn stones into bread to satisfy his hunger. Jesus prevails where Israel had succumbed.

Israel's second great sin in the forty-year desert wanderings was presuming to put the Lord to the test. At the slightest setback they demanded that God prove himself to them all over again, even though the deliverance from Egypt was still in living memory! Moses scolded them for this, too. As the book of Deuteronomy records:

> Do not put the LORD your God to the test as you did at Massah
> [where they demanded fresh signs from God]. (Deuteronomy 6:16)

When Jesus was urged to throw himself off the highest point of the temple to test God's faithfulness to him, he quoted these very words of Moses in response. Again, Jesus proves faithful where Israel had proved faithless.

The third and most tragic of Israel's failures in the desert was, as I mentioned earlier, their worship of pagan deities. They made the mistake at least twice during the forty-year wanderings (Exodus 32:1–6; Numbers 25:1–3) and Moses pleaded with them:

> Be careful that you do not forget the LORD, who brought you
> out of Egypt, out of the land of slavery. Fear the LORD your
> God, serve him only. . . . Do not follow other gods, the gods
> of the peoples around you. (Deuteronomy 6:12–14)

Jesus quotes these very words when faced with a similar temptation. According to Matthew's Gospel, the devil took Jesus to a high mountain and "showed him all the kingdoms of the world." (Incidentally, this is why I think the narrative describes a visionary experience rather than some kind of satanic teleportation. There is obviously no vantage point from which one can view "all the kingdoms" of the world.) All of this could be yours, says the devil to Jesus, if only you worship me. Jesus does no such thing. Instead, he quotes Moses, remaining firm in his resolve to "serve God only." Yet again, where Israel had so tragically failed, Jesus—the new son of God—prevailed.

For Matthew's first readers this was evocative stuff. Every Jew knew that Israel's sins in the desert had been an ominous foreshadowing of the failures that would characterise the entire history of the nation. The desert sins were the beginning of the end for Israel's national and religious life. By submitting himself to a forty-day desert trial in which he would withstand the very temptations which had ruined Israel, Jesus was enacting a very powerful message for his Jewish brothers and sisters: *in Christ, God's people can enjoy a new beginning, a rewriting of the tragic story of Israel.* The call to follow Jesus, then, which we hear for the first time just a few paragraphs later in the Gospels, is an invitation to break out of the previous story, with its cycle of sin and judgment, and enter into a new story—a new "exodus" from slavery—and join a revived "Israel," a new people of God.

## JESUS AND THE TWELVE NEW TRIBES OF ISRAEL

According to all four Gospels, the call to follow Christ was first taken up by a small group of men whom Jesus designated "apostles" (meaning "sent ones"). The choice of these individuals was again informed by the ancient story of Israel. Let me quote the relevant passage in Mark's Gospel and then explain what I mean:

> Jesus went up on a mountainside and called to him those he wanted, and they came to him. He appointed twelve [—designating them apostles—] that they might be with him and that he might send them out to preach and to have authority to drive out demons. These are the twelve he appointed: Simon (to whom he gave the name Peter), James son of Zebedee and his brother John (to them he gave the name Boanerges, which means "sons of thunder"), Andrew, Philip, Bartholomew, Matthew, Thomas, James son of Alphaeus, Thaddaeus, Simon the Zealot and Judas Iscariot, who betrayed him. (Mark 3:13–19)

In light of the theme we have been exploring, it cannot be an accident that Jesus selected, and then commissioned, exactly *twelve* apostles. In the history of Israel the number twelve had a unique significance. It was the number of sons born to Abraham's grandson, Jacob (aka "Israel"); it was thus the number of tribes in the chosen nation. For Jews, "twelve" always recalled the full complement of God's people, as is clear in many Old Testament passages (e.g., Genesis 17:20; Exodus 28:21; Numbers 17:1–3; Joshua 4:1–7).

A saying of Jesus found in Matthew and Luke (from their earlier shared source, Q) makes explicit this connection between the apostles and the twelve tribes of Israel. Jesus is here speaking about the future kingdom of God (discussed in the previous chapter) and the place of the apostles in it:

> Peter answered him, "We have left everything to follow you!
> What then will there be for us?" Jesus said to them, "Truly
> I tell you, at the renewal of all things, when the Son of Man
> [i.e., Jesus] sits on his glorious throne, you who have followed
> me will also sit on twelve thrones, judging the twelve tribes
> of Israel." (Matthew 19:27–28)

All mainstream biblical historians affirm the fact and significance of Jesus' choice of twelve founding delegates. Professor Graham Stanton of the University of Cambridge sums up the scholarly consensus well:

> What is the significance of the number twelve? Jesus' choice
> of this number provides an important clue to his intentions:
> the twelve were chosen by Jesus as the nucleus of the "true" or
> "restored" twelve tribes of Israel which he sought to establish . . .
> The importance of the call of the twelve can scarcely be
> exaggerated. In this prophetic action Jesus is calling for the
> renewal of Israel. He is also expressing the conviction that
> God is now beginning to establish anew his people—and
> will bring this promise to fulfillment. (Stanton, *The Gospels
> and Jesus*, 201.)

Jesus' miniature "exodus" from Egypt and his reenactment of Israel's "desert wanderings" point in precisely the same direction as his selection of the twelve leaders of his new movement. Jesus was signalling to those around him that through his ministry God was rewriting the story of his ancient people. The time of disobedience and judgment was over; the period of renewal had begun.

# REFLECTIONS

Readers may be wondering whether such a historically specific aspect of Christ's life could have any relevance outside the context of first-century Israel. A few points are worth mentioning.

## Anti-Semitism

I should clarify that Jesus' vision of the rewriting of Israel's story was not born out of anti-Semitism. Jesus was a Jew, after all! He longed for the renewal of Israel not its extinction. The long line of eminent *Jewish* scholars writing about the historical Jesus makes this point perfectly clear: Joseph Klausner, David Flusser, Pinchas Lapide, Geza Vermes, Paula Fredriksen, and others.

In the history of the Christian church this point has sometimes been too little appreciated. The portrayal of Jews as "Christ-killers," whose place in God's affections was supplanted by the church (a widespread Protestant viewpoint in sixteenth- to twentieth-century Europe), has no basis in the New Testament. Any Protestants who think I am being unfair at this point should take the time to read the reformer Martin Luther's 1543 publication "The Jews and Their Lies," easily read with a quick online search, or in *Luther's Works*, vol. 38 (Philadelphia: Fortress, 1971, 268–93). How Luther ever wrote this document when he had New Testament passages like Romans 9:1–5 and 11:1–32 in front of him is a mystery (and Romans was his favourite biblical book!).

The theological relationship between the Christian church and the Jewish community is, frankly, a mystery: in fact, "mystery" is exactly the word used in Romans 11:25–32 to describe the relationship. But one thing is clear: for all his criticisms of his fellow

Israelites, the historical Jesus was intent on inviting the chosen people to find in him all that their ancient Scriptures had promised.

## Jesus as the Representative of God's People

What is the relevance of all this for those outside of Jesus' first hearers? At this point I hope readers will permit me to do a bit of theology. According to the rest of the New Testament, Jesus (the ideal Israel) is the one who represents God's people before the Almighty himself. Here we arrive at a subtle but potent biblical theme, one that Christians down through the ages have cherished. *Jesus performed the obedience throughout his life that we in our frailty (just like ancient Israel) could never fully offer.*

According to the New Testament, Christ's obedience is the obedience God accepts on behalf of others. What he did—from his successful forty-day trial to his final breath—is counted as the faithfulness of all who follow him. He is our priest and representative. This is exactly how one book in the New Testament, aptly titled Hebrews, describes Jesus' (desert) temptations. The passage is complex, but the central point is clear:

> Therefore, since we have a great high priest who has ascended into heaven, Jesus the Son of God, let us hold firmly to the faith we profess. For we do not have a high priest who is unable to empathize with our weaknesses, but we have one who has been tempted in every way, just as we are—yet he did not sin [probably a reference to the desert temptations]. . . . Son though he was, he learned obedience from what he suffered and, once made perfect, he became the source of eternal salvation for all who obey him and was designated by God to

be high priest in the order of Melchizedek. We have much to say about this, but it is hard to make it clear to you because you no longer try to understand. (Hebrews 4:14–15; 5:8–11)

I would not want to echo the sentiment of the final clause, but I would like to emphasise the writer's main point: Jesus' obedience (from his wilderness temptations to his death) is the full obedience none of us is able to offer the Creator. As the priest who represents us to God, his obedience is the source of salvation for all who obey him, even though their obedience will only ever be a dim reflection of his.

As I was writing this chapter a friend expressed a common contemporary response to Christ's message: "But sometimes it's so difficult," she said. "He set the bar so high, I don't know if I can do it." At one level, this is an appropriate response to Christ's demands—his teaching discussed in chapter 2 has deep implications for the whole of life. But it must be balanced, as I explained to my friend, with knowing that, according to the New Testament, Jesus' fully obedient life (and death) more than makes up for our frequently disobedient lives. As another New Testament writer put it:

But if anybody does sin, we have an advocate with the Father— Jesus Christ, the Righteous One. He is the atoning sacrifice for our sins. (1 John 2:1–2)

Put another way, believers live out their imperfect stories within the larger perfect story of the Righteous One. Following him, however imperfectly, is perfect membership in God's new Israel.

## The Model of Obedience

So long as we remember that our standing before God is dependent on Jesus' obedience, not our own, it is entirely appropriate to view the Christian life as being fundamentally about trying to do what Jesus did—to be like him. The deeds we perform are not the means of writing ourselves into God's good books, but they are the obvious consequence of knowing that we have been written into that book already.

Followers of Christ daily try to copy Jesus' story into their own life story. Like him, they try to resist the temptation to grumble at God's provision. They remind themselves that man does not live by bread (and BMWs) alone. Like him, they say no to putting God to the test by demanding signs from him and insisting that he do things their way, and so on. Like him, they refuse to bow down to the gods of their age—to the dollar, the body, the never-ending renovation. They say with Jesus, "Worship the Lord your God, and serve him only."

As the new Israel, Jesus *represents* his people before God. As the new Israel, Jesus *models* what it means to live as the people of God. The Christian life is lived out within these twin realities of what Jesus did on our behalf and what he showed us to do.

## A SELECTION OF READINGS FROM THE OLD TESTAMENT OR JEWISH SCRIPTURES

## God Calls Abraham, the First "Jew," to Found a Great Nation and Bless All Nations

This is the account of Terah's family line. Terah became the father of Abram, Nahor and Haran. And Haran became the father of Lot. While his father Terah was still alive, Haran died in Ur of the Chaldeans, in the land of his birth. Abram and Nahor both married. The name of Abram's wife was Sarai, and the name of Nahor's wife was Milkah; she was the daughter of Haran, the father of both Milkah and Iskah. Now Sarai was childless because she was not able to conceive. Terah took his son Abram, his grandson Lot son of Haran, and his daughter-in-law Sarai, the wife of his son Abram, and together they set out from Ur of the Chaldeans to go to Canaan. But when they came to Harran, they settled there. Terah lived 205 years, and he died in Harran. The Lord had said to Abram, "Go from your country, your people and your father's household to the land I will show you. I will make you into a great nation, and I will bless you; I will make your name great, and you will be a blessing. I will bless those who bless you, and whoever curses you I will curse; and all peoples on earth will be blessed through you." So Abram went, as the Lord had told him; and Lot went with him. Abram was seventy-five years old when he set out from Harran. He took his wife Sarai, his nephew Lot, all the possessions they had accumulated and the people they had acquired in Harran, and they set out for the land of Canaan, and they arrived there. Abram traveled through the land as far as the site of the great tree of Moreh at Shechem. At that time the Canaanites were in the land. The LORD appeared to Abram and said, "To your offspring I will give this land." So he built an altar there to the LORD, who had appeared to him. (Genesis 11:27–12:7)

## The Passover and Exodus from Egypt

The LORD said to Moses and Aaron in Egypt, "This month is to be for you the first month, the first month of your year. Tell the whole community of Israel that on the tenth day of this month each man is to take a lamb for his family, one for each household. If any household is too small for a whole lamb, they must share one with their nearest neighbor, having taken into account the number of people there are. You are to determine the amount of lamb needed in accordance with what each person will eat. The animals you choose must be year-old males without defect, and you may take them from the sheep or the goats. Take care of them until the fourteenth day of the month, when all the members of the community of Israel must slaughter them at twilight. Then they are to take some of the blood and put it on the sides and tops of the doorframes of the houses where they eat the lambs. That same night they are to eat the meat roasted over the fire, along with bitter herbs, and bread made without yeast. Do not eat the meat raw or boiled in water, but roast it over a fire—with the head, legs and internal organs. Do not leave any of it till morning; if some is left till morning, you must burn it. This is how you are to eat it: with your cloak tucked into your belt, your sandals on your feet and your staff in your hand. Eat it in haste; it is the LORD's Passover. On that same night I will pass through Egypt and strike down every firstborn of both people and animals, and I will bring judgment on all the gods of Egypt. I am the Lord. The blood will be a sign for you on the houses where you are, and when I see the blood, I will pass over you. No destructive plague will touch you when I strike Egypt. This is a day you are to commemorate; for the generations to come you shall celebrate it as a festival to the Lord—a lasting ordinance." (Exodus 12:1–14)

## The Famous Ten Commandments of Moses

I am the Lord your God, who brought you out of Egypt, out of the land of slavery. You shall have no other gods before me. You shall not make for yourself an image in the form of anything in heaven above or on the earth beneath or in the waters below. You shall not bow down to them or worship them; for I, the Lord your God, am a jealous God, punishing the children for the sin of the parents to the third and fourth generation of those who hate me, but showing love to a thousand generations of those who love me and keep my commandments. You shall not misuse the name of the Lord your God, for the Lord will not hold anyone guiltless who misuses his name. Observe the Sabbath day by keeping it holy, as the Lord your God has commanded you. Six days you shall labor and do all your work, but the seventh day is a sabbath to the Lord your God. On it you shall not do any work, neither you, nor your son or daughter, nor your male or female servant, nor your ox, your donkey or any of your animals, nor any foreigner residing in your towns, so that your male and female servants may rest, as you do. Remember that you were slaves in Egypt and that the Lord your God brought you out of there with a mighty hand and an outstretched arm. Therefore the LORD your God has commanded you to observe the Sabbath day. Honor your father and your mother, as the LORD your God has commanded you, so that you may live long and that it may go well with you in the land the LORD your God is giving you. You shall not murder. You shall not commit adultery. You shall not steal. You shall not give false testimony against your neighbor. You shall not covet your neighbor's wife. You shall not set your desire on your neighbor's house or land, his male or female servant, his ox or donkey, or anything that belongs to your neighbor. (Deuteronomy 5:6–21)

## A Prophecy About the Coming Messiah

Nevertheless, there will be no more gloom for those who were in distress. In the past he humbled the land of Zebulun and the land of Naphtali, but in the future he will honor Galilee of the nations, by the Way of the Sea, beyond the Jordan—The people walking in darkness have seen a great light; on those living in the land of deep darkness a light has dawned. You have enlarged the nation and increased their joy; they rejoice before you as people rejoice at the harvest, as warriors rejoice when dividing the plunder. For as in the day of Midian's defeat, you have shattered the yoke that burdens them, the bar across their shoulders, the rod of their oppressor. Every warrior's boot used in battle and every garment rolled in blood will be destined for burning, will be fuel for the fire. For to us a child is born, to us a son is given, and the government will be on his shoulders. And he will be called Wonderful Counselor, Mighty God, Everlasting Father, Prince of Peace. Of the greatness of his government and peace there will be no end. He will reign on David's throne and over his kingdom, establishing and upholding it with justice and righteousness from that time on and forever. The zeal of the LORD Almighty will accomplish this. (Isaiah 9:1–7)

## Ezekiel's Marriage-Adultery Parable of the History of Israel

The word of the LORD came to me: "Son of man, confront Jerusalem with her detestable practices and say, 'This is what the Sovereign LORD says to Jerusalem: Your ancestry and birth were in the land of the Canaanites; your father was an Amorite and your mother a Hittite. On the day you were born your cord was not cut, nor were you washed with water to make you clean, nor were you rubbed with salt or wrapped in cloths. No one looked on you with pity or had compassion enough to do any of these things for you. Rather, you were thrown out into the open field, for on the day you were born you were despised. Then I passed by and saw you kicking about in your blood, and as you lay there in your blood I said to you, 'Live!' I made you grow like a plant of the field. You grew and developed and entered puberty. Your breasts had formed and your hair had grown, yet you were stark naked. Later I passed by, and when I looked at you and saw that you were old enough for love, I spread the corner of my garment over you and covered your naked body. I gave you my solemn oath and entered into a covenant with you, declares the Sovereign LORD, and you became mine. I bathed you with water and washed the blood from you and put ointments on you. I clothed you with an embroidered dress and put sandals of fine leather on you. I dressed you in fine linen and covered you with costly garments. I adorned you with jewelry: I put bracelets on your arms and a necklace around your neck, and I put a ring on your nose, earrings on your ears and a beautiful crown on your head. So you were adorned with gold and silver; your clothes were of fine linen and costly fabric and embroidered cloth. Your food was honey, olive oil and the finest flour. You became very beautiful and rose to be a queen. And your fame spread among the nations on account of your beauty, because the splendor I had given you made your beauty perfect, declares the Sovereign LORD. But you trusted in your beauty and used your fame to become a prostitute. You lavished your favors on anyone who passed by and your beauty became his. You took some of your garments to make gaudy high places, where you carried on your prostitution. You went to him, and he possessed your beauty. You also took the fine jewelry I gave you, the jewelry made of my gold and silver, and you made for yourself male idols and engaged in prostitution with them. And you took your embroidered clothes to put on them, and you offered my oil and incense before them. Also the food I provided for you—the flour, olive oil and honey I gave you to eat—you offered as fragrant incense before them. That is what happened, declares the Sovereign LORD." (Ezekiel 16:1–19)

# 6

## CHRIST:

## MORE THAN A SURNAME

Some people grow up—I admit to being one of them—with the impression that "Christ" was the surname of Jesus. But, of course, "Christ" was a prestigious title, and one of central importance to two world religions, not just one.

### THE "CHRIST" OF TRADITIONAL JUDAISM

To this day, observant Jews pray earnestly for the ruler promised in their Scriptures (the Tanak or Old Testament), descended from King David (1000 BC), who would liberate Israel from its enemies and establish the kingdom of God in the world. Each day of the week, our Orthodox Jewish neighbours recite words that have been part of Judaism since ancient times. The prayer, from the *Siddur* (or Jewish Prayer Book), pleads:

> The offspring of Your servant David may You speedily cause to flourish, and enhance his glory through Your salvation, for we hope for Your salvation all day long. (*Shemoneh Esreh*

15 in *The Complete ArtScroll Siddur*. New York: Mesorah
Publications, 2001)

Another prayer for this promised king appears (again in the *Siddur*)
in the Jewish equivalent of a "grace" said after meal times every
mid-week day:

Have mercy, our God, on Israel Your people; on Jerusalem,
Your city, on Zion, the resting place of Your Glory; on the
monarchy of the house of David, Your Anointed. (*Rahem*,
Third Blessing after Meals)

The all-important word here, "Anointed," translates the Hebrew
term *mashiach*. The term is anglicized as "Messiah." The equivalent
in the Greek language of the New Testament is *christos*, which is
anglicized as "Christ." In other words, "Messiah" and "Christ" both
refer to the king *anointed* by God to rule on his behalf.

The idea of anointed kings—of messiahs or christs—goes
right back to the time of the biblical prophet Samuel 1000 years
before Jesus. The most significant of all of Samuel's duties was to
commission, by anointing, a young shepherd boy named David
(of David and Goliath fame):

The LORD said to Samuel, "Fill your horn with oil and be
on your way; I am sending you to Jesse of Bethlehem. I have
chosen one of his sons to be king." . . . Then the LORD said,
"Rise and anoint him; this is the one." So Samuel took the
horn of oil and anointed him in the presence of his brothers,

and from that day on the Spirit of the LORD came powerfully upon David. (1 Samuel 16:1, 12–13)

King David was not the first or last person in the Bible to undergo an anointing ceremony, but he was considered the model of a king anointed with God's Spirit and power. He was, if you like, the first messiah, the first christ.

The central importance of David for the notion of an ultimate future messiah-christ was fixed forever in Jewish belief because of a prophecy given to King David by the prophet, Nathan, Samuel's successor. According to the prophecy, David's kingdom would somehow reign forever:

When your days are over and you rest with your ancestors, I will raise up your offspring to succeed you, your own flesh and blood, and I will establish his kingdom. . . . Your house and your kingdom will endure forever before me; your throne will be established forever. (2 Samuel 7:12, 16)

It is impossible to overstate the importance of these words for both Judaism and Christianity. The hope for an eternal kingdom established by God, and administered by a descendant of King David, is at the heart of Jewish and Christian hope.

Even when David's four-hundred-year historical dynasty collapsed in the sixth century BC, the Israelites clung to this ancient prophecy as their great hope. The prophets during this period of Israel's demise reiterated this ancient promise by insisting that out of the "stump" of David's fallen family tree would emerge a spirit-anointed king who would fulfil the hopes of Israel and govern the world forever. Consider this promise in the Old Testament book of Isaiah:

> A shoot will come up from the stump of Jesse [David's
>     family name];
>     from his roots a Branch will bear fruit.
> The Spirit of the LORD will rest on him. . . .
> He will not judge by what he sees with his eyes,
>     or decide by what he hears with his ears;
> but with righteousness he will judge the needy,
>         with justice he will give decisions for the poor of
>             the earth.
> He will strike the earth with the rod of his mouth;
>         with the breath of his lips he will slay the wicked. . . .
> In that day the Root of Jesse will stand as a banner for the
> peoples; the nations will rally to him, and his resting place
> will be glorious. (Isaiah 11:1–4, 10)

This is the anointed king Jews long for daily in the words: "Have mercy, our God . . . on the monarchy of the house of David, Your Anointed." Please fulfil your promise, dear Lord, say Orthodox Jews each morning and at meal times; send us your messiah-christ, the banner for all nations.

## THE CHRIST OF CHRISTIANITY

Only when we understand this deep Jewish longing for the Davidic messiah will we appreciate the enormity and scandal of the Gospels' emphatic claim that this anointed one is to be found in the teacher and healer from Nazareth. Matthew begins his Gospel with the words:

> This is the genealogy of Jesus the Messiah the son of David (Matthew 1:1).

The central paragraph of Mark's Gospel records:

> "But what about you?" he [Jesus] asked. "Who do you say I am?" Peter answered, "You are the Messiah." (Mark 8:29)

In Luke's Gospel, Jesus' trial revolves around this claim:

> We have found this man subverting our nation. He opposes payment of taxes to Caesar and claims to be Messiah, a king. (Luke 23:2)

The summary at the end of John's Gospel states bluntly:

> But these [things] are written that you may believe that Jesus is the Messiah. (John 20:31)

Historically speaking, more important than all of these quotations from the Gospels is the fact that our earliest Christian writings, the letters of the apostle Paul, refer to Jesus as "Christ" or "Messiah" literally hundreds of times. What's more, many of these appear without the definite article: he is simply "Christ" rather than "*the* Christ." For the historian, this is significant. It indicates that as early as the AD 40s the title Christ/Messiah was so closely associated with Jesus that it was almost being used as his name, not just his title. This may seem like an insignificant detail, but it gives historians pause. It was once argued by scholars that Jesus' Messiah status was only proposed in the decades after his death, that it was not the view of his first followers and certainly not the view of Jesus himself. The Gospel writers, these critics said, wrote a Messiah story *back into* their presentation of Jesus. Without Paul's letters this argument might just have worked (though it would face many historical hurdles from the Gospels). However, the fact that the title Christ had already begun to morph into a kind of surname within a few years of Jesus' death suggests that the practice of calling Jesus *the Messiah* must have begun even earlier, with his immediate circle of followers. (The more daring among my readers may wish to read a full scholarly account of this point, by the British New Testament expert N. T. Wright in his monumental *The Resurrection of the Son of God*. London: SPCK, 2004, 553–63.)

It is no exaggeration to say that the central claim about Jesus in earliest Christianity was that he was the promised Christ or Messiah. More than a teacher or healer or the new Israel, Jesus was announced to all as the descendant of King David, anointed by God to fulfil the hopes of Israel, and to "rally the nations" under his command, just as the ancient prophecy of Isaiah 11:10 quoted earlier had promised.

Interestingly, these claims were heard and reported by non-Christian writers of the period as well. The Roman writers Suetonius and Tacitus refer to Jesus as "Christ," even though they would have had little idea of what the title implied. The first-century Jewish historian Josephus describes Jesus in words that apparently did not come easily off the pen. When he narrates the martyrdom of Jesus' brother James, Josephus uses a somewhat awkward expression: "he [Ananus the High Priest] convened the judges of the Sanhedrin and brought before them a man named James, the brother of Jesus who was called the Christ" (*Jewish Antiquities* 20.200). As many specialists point out, Josephus's exact words here—*legomenos Christos*—may mean "so-called Christ," hinting at his personal reservation about the claim that Jesus was Messiah. Josephus did not endorse Jesus as the Messiah, but his words confirm that in the first century the principal claim about Jesus, heard far and wide, was that he was the Christ, God's anointed king over the nations.

## JESUS AND THE MESSIANIC JOB DESCRIPTION

But why, we may ask, were only tens of thousands of Jews convinced by Jesus' claims, instead of hundreds of thousands or even millions? (There may have been between 5 and 8 million Jews in the first century, most of whom lived outside the land of Israel.) There are certainly socio-political factors we could talk about, but the principal reason probably lies in the fact that Jesus did not fit the job description expected of a messiah in first-century Galilee and Judaea. Recall the messianic prophecy of Isaiah quoted earlier:

He will not judge by what he sees with his eyes,
    or decide by what he hears with his ears;
but with righteousness he will judge the needy,
    with justice he will give decisions for the poor of
        the earth.
He will strike the earth with the rod of his mouth;
    with the breath of his lips he will slay the wicked. . . .

> In that day the Root of Jesse will stand as a banner for the peoples; the nations will rally to him, and his resting place will be glorious. (Isaiah 11:3–4, 10)

In Jesus' day, this messianic language was interpreted in military terms. The "needy" and "poor" were of course the Jews; the "wicked" were the Romans who ruled Judaea from 63 BC; and the messiah's "mouth" and "breath" were his commands to slay Israel's enemies. The "rallying" of the nations mentioned here was nothing less than the world's final submission to a Jewish king.

The alternative interpretation (offered by the followers of Jesus) was not widely considered: the "needy" are all who need God; the "wicked" are all who do injustice; the Messiah's "mouth" and "breath" are simply his world-conquering teaching; and the "rallying" of the nations to him is the world's willing acceptance of him as history's true Lord. Given some hindsight, there can be little doubt that Jesus of Nazareth fits this second interpretation well. Within three centuries the Roman Empire was indeed bowing the knee to the teaching of Christ. Today Jesus is revered as Christ in more than two thousand languages amongst more than two billion people scattered across all the nations of the world.

Of course, hindsight is a beautiful thing. In the first century, worldwide devotion to a Jewish teacher was not what the Jews hoped for when they looked at their ancient prophecies. Many (not all) longed for a *military* messiah, one who would crush Israel's enemies by divine force. Evidence of this expectation is found not only in the numerous anti-Roman Jewish movements we know of from the period but also in some of the pious texts composed around the time of Jesus.

Around 50 BC, just a decade or so after Pompey's Roman armies marched onto Israel's sacred soil, a Jewish leader in Jerusalem wrote a prayer pleading God to send a particular kind of messiah. In short, he wanted a military commander descended from David who would smash the foreigners to pieces:

> See, O Lord, and raise up for them [the Jewish people] their king, the son of David, to rule over your servant Israel in the time known to you, O God. Undergird him with the strength to destroy the unrighteous rulers [the Romans], to purge Jerusalem from gentiles who trample her to destruction; in wisdom and in righteousness to drive out the sinners from the inheritance; to smash the arrogance of sinners like a potter's jar. There will be no unrighteousness among them in his days, for all shall be holy, and their king shall be the Lord Messiah. (R. B. Wright, "Psalms of Solomon." In vol. 2 of *Old Testament Pseudepigrapha.* Edited by James Charlesworth. New York: Doubleday, 1985, 667.)

Clearly, the "Lord Messiah" described in this text is different from the figure we find in the pages of the Gospels. This messiah would "smash" the sinners; Jesus offered sinners forgiveness and transformation (as we will see in chapter 7). This messiah would lead a successful rebellion against the foreign invaders; Jesus said "love your enemies, do good to them" (Luke 6:35). Jesus did not fit any messianic job description we know of from the period, and some of his teachings ran counter to the little we do know about first-century aspirations.

This insight in part solves one of the puzzles in the Gospels. Scholars have often wondered why Jesus was so cagey about publicly accepting the title Messiah/Christ—he occasionally even told people not to spread the word about him (Mark 1:43–44; 8:29–30). One explanation of this feature, made plausible in light of the above passage, is that Jesus did not want people to associate him with the kind of messiah expected in Jerusalem at the time. Only when it was crystal clear that he had not come to "destroy the unrighteous rulers" would he allow the title Messiah to be connected with his ministry.

---

**BOOK NOTES** | For a brief and reliable account of the concept of "Messiah/Christ" in Jewish expectation, see Joel B. Green, "Christ, Messiah." *The Routledge Encyclopedia of the Historical Jesus.* Edited by Craig A. Evans. London: Routledge, 2008, 101–7.

---

## THE PEOPLE OF THE MESSIAH

In the central passage of Mark's Gospel, taken up by Luke and Matthew as well, Jesus describes what embracing his version of the messiah will involve. To set the scene, it is perhaps halfway through Jesus' three-year public career as a teacher and healer. He stops and asks his twelve apostles *who* they think they have been travelling with for the last eighteen months or so. The episode is both a climax and an anti-climax:

"But what about you?" he asked. "Who do you say I am?"
Peter answered, "You are the Messiah." Jesus warned them

not to tell anyone about him. He then began to teach them
that the Son of Man [Jesus] must suffer many things and be
rejected by the elders, the chief priests and the teachers of
the law, and that he must be killed and after three days rise
again. He spoke plainly about this, and Peter took him aside
and began to rebuke him. But when Jesus turned and looked
at his disciples, he rebuked Peter. "Get behind me, Satan!"
he said. "You do not have in mind the concerns of God, but
merely human concerns."

Then he called the crowd to him along with his disciples
and said: "Whoever wants to be my disciple must deny
themselves and take up their cross and follow me. For whoever wants to save their life will lose it, but whoever loses
their life for me and for the gospel will save it. What good is
it for someone to gain the whole world, yet forfeit their soul?
Or what can anyone give in exchange for their soul? If anyone is ashamed of me and my words in this adulterous and
sinful generation, the Son of Man will be ashamed of them
when he comes in his Father's glory with the holy angels."
(Mark 8:29–38)

Here it is clear that Jesus' messianic mission is not to "purge
Jerusalem from gentiles," as the Jewish text quoted earlier suggested,
but to suffer, die, and rise again. With almost two thousand years
of Christianisation, in a way it is difficult for modern readers to
appreciate just how shocking this notion of a suffering messiah
would have been. We catch a glimpse of it in the response of the
chief apostle, Peter, who took his master aside and "rebuked" him.
Jesus responds with his own stinging rebuke contrasting human

ambitions for the messiah with those of God: "You do not have in mind the concerns of God," he says to Peter, "but merely human concerns."

So great is Peter's misunderstanding of the messiah's mission that Jesus calls the crowd together in the second paragraph just quoted and makes clear that following him will not involve gaining the world; instead, it means taking up a cross. The contrast here is between two ways of being the people of the messiah. The first tries to protect its interests and "gain the whole world." In historical context, this is not a reference to materialism but to messianic imperialism—the attempt to dominate the nations. It was what Jesus himself was offered in the devilish vision of his temptation discussed in the previous chapter. Such a path, says Jesus, will result in the loss of one's soul before God.

The true way of belonging to the messiah involves denying such ambitions and deciding to follow Jesus and his words wherever they lead—to loving one's enemies, doing good to one's persecutors, and even to a cross. The climactic words about being "ashamed of me and my words in this adulterous and sinful generation" have little to do with Christians feeling shy about their faith in a secular world. In the original setting they must have meant that following a crucified messiah in a conquest-culture would bring public shame. Disciples must be willing to bear this.

In short, Jesus appears to have demanded that people give up their private preferences and interpretations of what following the messiah means and entrust themselves to him utterly, wherever it leads. Being the people of the messiah involves absolute, unconditional loyalty to the one whom God has anointed as the rallying point for the nations.

## REFLECTIONS

For the first few hundred years of Christian history, bearing the name of "Christ"—as the word "Christian" entailed—was a risky business. A year or so after Jesus' death, a leader of the Greek-speaking disciples in Jerusalem, named Stephen, was put to death by stoning (Acts 7:54–60; AD 31/32). In AD 42 the first of the twelve apostles, James son of Zebedee, was likewise martyred, this time by beheading (Acts 12:1–2). After a period of relative calm, the AD 60s saw the killing of James the brother of Jesus (Josephus, *Jewish Antiquities* 20.200; AD 62), the apostles Peter and Paul (1 Clement 5:1–7; Eusebius, *Ecclesiastical History* 2.25.5–6; AD 64/65), and scores of unnamed disciples whose dreadful fate under Nero's reign (AD 54–68) even made the Roman official Tacitus (AD 56–120) wince.

> The confessed members of the sect were arrested; next, on their disclosures, vast numbers were convicted. . . . And derision accompanied their end: they were covered with wild beasts' skins and torn to death by dogs; or they were fastened on crosses, and, when daylight failed were burned to serve as lamps by night. Nero had offered his Gardens for the spectacle, and gave an exhibition in his Circus, mixing with the crowd in the habit of a charioteer, or mounted on his car. Hence, in spite of a guilt which had earned the most exemplary punishment, there arose a sentiment of pity, due to the impression that they were being sacrificed not for the welfare of the state but to the ferocity of a single man [Nero]. (Tacitus, *Annals* 15.44)

The words of Mark 8:34, "If anyone would come after me, let him deny himself and take up his cross and follow me" (ESV), must have had special resonance for the first followers of Jesus. They had watched their "king" suffer and die, and now they were required to walk the same path.

It must have been tempting at times to take matters into their own hands—as, unfortunately, the church of a later time did—and seek to establish the Messiah's kingdom by force. But the early disciples knew, against all the currents of their society, that this was not the way of God and his Anointed One. Christians of this period bore the name (and the shame) of their king whatever the outcome.

The modern church would do well to remember this lesson when it too is tempted to establish itself in society by force (whether political or military). It would do well to heed the warning of the Messiah himself: "What good is it for someone to gain the whole world, yet forfeit their soul?" (Mark 8:36).

In February 2015 twenty-one Coptic Christians were executed by ISIS on a Libyan beach. It received worldwide attention, for a moment. Less well known is that the brother of two of the young men was interviewed on Egyptian Christian TV channel Sat-7. His name is Beshir and he thanked the extremists for leaving the sound *on* in the propaganda video of the beheadings. The video went viral around the Middle East. Many of the victims could be heard praying to and declaring their faith in "the Lord Jesus Christ." They are a "badge of honour to Christianity," said Beshir. "Since the Roman era," he continued, "Christians have been martyred and have learned to handle everything that comes our way. It only makes us stronger in our faith because the Bible tells us to love our enemies and bless those who curse us." (For the initial reports, see: http://www.bbc.com/news/world-middle-east-31490089. For the interview with Beshir, see: http://www.christiantoday.com/article/brother.of.slain.coptic.christians.thanks.isis.for.including.their.words.of.faith.in.murder.video/48412.htm.)

It is tragically ironic that the church of the West has come to be seen by many as an institution that misuses power. This is partly the world's bias. The church is a big organization, with a long history, out of step with society at some points. It's an easy target. But Christians don't help themselves when they speak in public with an air of entitlement, allowing boldness to morph into simple arrogance.

How can Christians possibly hope to convince Westerners that Jesus Christ came to serve, suffer, and save them, if they are thought of as bullying, grumbling, and grasping for cultural ground? Only when the followers of Christ are known for denying themselves and taking up their public "crosses" will they begin to look like the One they claim to represent.

# 7

## JUDGE:
### HIS PLEDGE TO BRING JUSTICE

Years ago, I was speaking to Year 10 students in a high school in Sydney's southwest. I asked them to imagine their life—every deed, word, and even thought—recorded on film and shown to family and friends. The awkwardness in the room was palpable. I then asked, rhetorically, "What if God could see that film and decided to hold it against us?" One young man in the audience, unaware my wife would overhear him, mumbled to himself, "I'd be stuffed" (an Australian colloquialism—bordering on a swear word—meaning "defeated").

This is not the most theologically articulate response I have heard, but it is instinctively appropriate. The thought that the Almighty knows our every thought, word, and deed, and that he has the right to hold us accountable, has caused most men and women over the millennia to reflect on their lives with seriousness and humility.

Nowadays people often object to any idea of God as wrathful. Part of the reason for this, I suspect, is a revulsion at the "fire and brimstone" preaching in some quarters of the church. An elderly friend of mine was put off church in her early thirties after hearing a series of very angry sermons about divine judgment. It seemed to Judy that the preacher enjoyed telling people of their impending doom. It was three decades before she took another look at the faith of her youth.

There is, of course, another reason people recoil from the concept of God's judgment: we simply do not like it. Cognitive dissonance theory in psychology tells us that when confronted by ideas that challenge our current assumptions, we tend to employ subconscious "defensive measures" to reduce the discomfort, including simply avoiding or explaining away the information. We manufacture beliefs to suit preferences. I am aware that this logic is sometimes thrown at religious people. "You want a father figure in the sky to help you cope with life," some skeptics might declare, "so you invent a deity to believe in." But the boot can just as easily be on the other foot. The inconvenience of the notion of the Almighty, especially one who might be displeased with the way I live, is a powerful motivator to exclude such a "god" from my thinking. It is not that such a god is inherently implausible or not in keeping with the facts; it simply does not suit my preference. The preferred God, for many in contemporary society, is the vague, distant Creator, the one who kicked off the universe but who now, if he thinks of us at all, warmly approves of most of what we do. Dissonance resolved.

This contemporary outlook makes it difficult for many today to approach, objectively, what is an unavoidable part of the historical portrait of Jesus of Nazareth. He regularly taught about divine judgment and even cast himself as the agent of that judgment. Before we look at the data concerning Jesus, I want to set his teaching within its biblical-historical context.

## DIVINE JUDGMENT AND LOVE IN THE BIBLE

Repeatedly and without embarrassment the Bible declares that the true God is a God of justice as well as love. In biblical thought the idea of judgment in no way contradicts the reality of divine love. The two are often spoken about together. It is no exaggeration to say that throughout the Bible God's judgment is frequently portrayed as a consequence, or even an aspect, of his compassion.

According to the Old Testament book of Exodus, God's concern for the enslaved Israelites is what moved him to overthrow their brutal Egyptian overlords. The turning point in the narrative reads:

> The Israelites groaned in their slavery and cried out, and their cry for help because of their slavery went up to God. God heard their groaning and he remembered his covenant with Abraham, with Isaac and with Jacob. So God looked on the Israelites and was concerned about them. (Exodus 2:23–25)

This was no simple divine favouritism. No sooner had God's people left Egypt than he gave them instructions about their own obligation to care for the downtrodden. If the Israelites oppressed the weak and poor, declared the Torah, they too would be overthrown:

> Do not mistreat or oppress a foreigner, for you were foreigners in Egypt. Do not take advantage of the widow or the fatherless. If you do and they cry out to me, I will certainly hear their cry. My anger will be aroused, and I will kill you with the sword; your wives will become widows and your children fatherless. (Exodus 22:21–24)

And five centuries later this is exactly what happened. The Assyrians ousted the Israelites "with the sword" and, according to the prophet Ezekiel (among others), this was largely because Israel had oppressed the needy within its borders:

> Her [Israel's] officials within her are like wolves tearing their prey; they shed blood and kill people to make unjust gain. Her prophets whitewash these deeds for them by false visions and lying divinations. They say, "This is what the Sovereign LORD says"—when the LORD has not spoken. The people of the land practice extortion and commit robbery; they oppress the poor and needy and mistreat the foreigner, denying them justice. I looked for someone among them who would build up the wall and stand before me in the gap on behalf of the land so I would not have to destroy it, but I found no one. So I will pour out my wrath on them and consume them with my fiery anger, bringing down on their own heads all they have done, declares the Sovereign LORD. (Ezekiel 22:27–31)

## HISTORY NOTE

Similar statements from Israel's prophets can be found in Isaiah 10:1–3, Jeremiah 2:31–37, Amos 5:1–27, and Zechariah 7:8–14. The other great sin that brought divine judgment down upon Israel was the worship of false gods. Both themes—Israel's idolatry and oppression of the needy—are frequently found together in the same prophetic denunciation (e.g., Jeremiah 2:26–37).

Not surprisingly, we observe the same connection between human injustice and divine judgment in the New Testament. For example, James the brother of Jesus insisted that God is so moved by the cries of the poor and defenceless that he will one day bring his wrath upon the rich oppressors of the world:

> Now listen, you rich people, weep and wail because of the misery that is coming on you. Your wealth has rotted, and moths have eaten your clothes. Your gold and silver are corroded. Their corrosion will testify against you and eat your flesh like fire. You have hoarded wealth in the last days. Look! The wages you failed to pay the workers who mowed your fields are crying out against you. The cries of the harvesters have reached the ears of the Lord Almighty. You have lived on earth in luxury and self-indulgence. You have fattened yourselves in the day of slaughter. You have condemned and murdered the innocent one, who was not opposing you. (James 5:1–6)

And, in what is perhaps the most disturbing of all the Bible's visions of future judgment, Revelation 18 describes the fate awaiting the city of Rome. Her obscene opulence while terrorising the innocent (including, no doubt, Nero's massacre of Christians in the AD 60s) makes her doubly suited for divine punishment:

> "'Woe! Woe to you, great city, where all who had ships on the sea became rich through her wealth! In one hour she has been brought to ruin!' Rejoice over her, you heavens! Rejoice, you people of God! Rejoice, apostles and prophets! For God has judged her with the judgment she imposed on you."

Then a mighty angel picked up a boulder the size of a large millstone and threw it into the sea, and said: "With such violence the great city of Babylon will be thrown down, never to be found again. The music of harpists and musicians, pipers and trumpeters, will never be heard in you again. No worker of any trade will ever be found in you again. The sound of a millstone will never be heard in you again. The light of a lamp will never shine in you again. The voice of bridegroom and bride will never be heard in you again. Your merchants were the world's important people. By your magic spell all the nations were led astray. In her was found the blood of prophets and of God's holy people, of all who have been slaughtered on the earth." (Revelation 18:19–24)

My point is simple: one of the most frequent and basic reasons given in the Bible for God's coming judgment is the reality of his compassion. God's fiery concern for the oppressed fuels his judgment upon oppressors.

## GOD'S JUDGMENT AND THE MESSIAH

Throughout the Bible, no individual is more closely associated with the execution of divine judgment than the coming Messiah. He is the one appointed by God to right the wrongs of the world. The Old Testament messianic prophecy of Isaiah 11 (quoted in the previous chapter) sums up the biblical perspective perfectly:

He will not judge by what he sees with his eyes,
    or decide by what he hears with his ears;
but with righteousness he will judge the needy,

with justice he will give decisions for the poor of the earth.
He will strike the earth with the rod of his mouth;
　　with the breath of his lips he will slay the wicked.

　　　　　　　　　　　　　　　　　　　　(Isaiah 11:3–4)

The Jewish Messiah, in other words, will be God's agent of judgment, defending the poor and overthrowing the unjust. He will embody God's fiery compassion for the oppressed and so execute God's judgment upon their oppressors.

Here we arrive at a frequently neglected, yet rather prominent, New Testament theme: the One entrusted with the judgment of the world is none other than Jesus, God's Messiah. There are so many passages we could reflect on. For instance, the apostle Peter declared in a sermon.

> He [Jesus] commanded us to preach to the people and to testify that he is the one whom God appointed as judge of the living and the dead. (Acts 10:42)

The apostle Paul said pretty much the same thing:

> This will take place on the day when God judges people's secrets through Jesus Christ, as my gospel declares. (Romans 2:16)

In an apocalyptic vision about the return of Jesus, John wrote in Revelation:

> I saw heaven standing open and there before me was a white horse, whose rider is called Faithful and True. With justice

he judges and wages war. . . . The armies of heaven were following him, riding on white horses and dressed in fine linen, white and clean. Coming out of his mouth is a sharp sword with which to strike down the nations. . . . He treads the winepress of the fury of the wrath of God Almighty. (Revelation 19:11, 14–15)

It would be easy to think that these New Testament writers were simply getting carried away with their own speculations about Jesus. In reality they were restating what they had heard from their Messiah's lips. By my count, there are close to a dozen occasions in the Gospels where Jesus affirms his role not only as the world's saviour—which we will look at in chapter 9—but also as its judge (e.g., Matthew 7:21–23; 13:36–43; Luke 13:22–30; John 5:25–30). Consider Jesus' words concerning certain Jewish towns that had rejected him and his message:

Woe to you, Chorazin! Woe to you, Bethsaida! For if the miracles that were performed in you had been performed in Tyre and Sidon [pagan cities], they would have repented long ago, sitting in sackcloth and ashes. But it will be more bearable for Tyre and Sidon at the judgment than for you. And you, Capernaum, will you be lifted to the heavens? No, you will go down to Hades. (Luke 10:13–15)

One could almost say that Jesus was the original "hell fire" preacher. The difference, of course, between him and the cliché some of us may have had the misfortune to endure is that Jesus delivered his message with a tear in his eye, not a smile on his face.

In a climactic scene of Luke's Gospel Jesus does in fact weep over a city, Jerusalem, that had rejected him (Luke 19:41–44).

One passage from Matthew's Gospel is especially interesting, for it reveals in the form of a parable both the agent of divine judgment and a central criterion of that judgment. Jesus' words are worth quoting in full:

> When the Son of Man comes in his glory, and all the angels with him, he will sit on his glorious throne. All the nations will be gathered before him, and he will separate the people one from another as a shepherd separates the sheep from the goats. He will put the sheep on his right and the goats on his left. Then the King will say to those on his right, "Come, you who are blessed by my Father; take your inheritance, the kingdom prepared for you since the creation of the world. For I was hungry and you gave me something to eat, I was thirsty and you gave me something to drink, I was a stranger and you invited me in, I needed clothes and you clothed me, I was sick and you looked after me, I was in prison and you came to visit me."
>
> Then the righteous will answer him, "Lord, when did we see you hungry and feed you, or thirsty and give you something to drink? When did we see you a stranger and invite you in, or needing clothes and clothe you? When did we see you sick or in prison and go to visit you?" The King will reply, "Truly I tell you, whatever you did for one of the least of these brothers and sisters of mine, you did for me."
>
> Then he will say to those on his left, "Depart from me, you who are cursed, into the eternal fire prepared for the devil and his angels. For I was hungry and you gave me nothing to

eat, I was thirsty and you gave me nothing to drink, I was a stranger and you did not invite me in, I needed clothes and you did not clothe me, I was sick and in prison and you did not look after me." They also will answer, "Lord, when did we see you hungry or thirsty or a stranger or needing clothes or sick or in prison, and did not help you?" He will reply, "Truly I tell you, whatever you did not do for one of the least of these, you did not do for me." Then they will go away to eternal punishment, but the righteous to eternal life. (Matthew 25:31–46)

Perfectly in line with the Old Testament prophecies about the Messiah, Jesus here declares that one day he will come in glory, sit on a heavenly throne (an image usually reserved for God alone, incidentally), and separate one person from another. He will speak the only words that will count on that day: "Come, you who are blessed" or alternatively "Depart from me, you who are cursed." I do not know what your mental picture of Jesus Christ is, but it must be said, if only as a historical statement, that without some place for Christ's claimed role as the divine Judge, our image of him is, to put it mildly, imprecise.

Personally, the idea of Jesus as Judge both comforts and troubles me. On the one hand, I am reassured to know that someone as compassionate as Christ is entrusted with the judgment of our flawed humanity. On the other hand, I am acutely aware that this same Jesus thundered against religious hypocrisy and railed against the neglect of the needy. As a member of wealthy Western Christendom, I admit to feeling somewhat in the firing line of this aspect of Christ's teaching.

This brings us to the criterion of judgment, according to the above passage. The thing separating the right from the left, the "sheep" from the "goats" or the "blessed" from the "cursed," is what they did or did not do, by action or neglect, for the plight of the destitute. Put positively, "I was hungry and you gave me something to eat . . ." Put negatively, "I was thirsty and you gave me nothing to drink." How we treat the needy, in other words, is how we treat their Defender and Judge, the Messiah. A central criterion of divine judgment, according to Jesus, is how we care for the destitute and exploited.

## HISTORY NOTE

Some Christian commentators have interpreted the mention of "brothers and sisters" in the above passage, "whatever you did for one of the least of these brothers and sisters," to mean that the followers of Christ are to assist only fellow believers. To my mind, that interpretation sails dangerously close to the kind of parochialism Jesus condemned in his famous Parable of the Good Samaritan (Luke 10:25–37), where he insisted that compassion is to be shown across the religious, social, and racial divide.

A couple of quick clarifications, and then I will bring this cheerless chapter to a close. First, Jesus is not suggesting in this passage that salvation from judgment is secured by the performance of charity. Read in isolation, I guess Matthew 25 could easily be taken that way. The problem is: there are too many other places in Jesus' teaching where he says that escaping divine wrath is a gift of divine mercy not a reward for good behaviour (among others see Luke 15:1–32; 18:9–14). The next chapter will underline this theme.

The quoted passage teaches what plenty of other New Testament texts teach: those who have received the gift of divine mercy commit themselves to lives of human mercy. The logic is summarised beautifully in Christ's words: "Be merciful, just as your Father God is merciful" (Luke 6:36). This connection between divine mercy and human mercy is so fundamental in Jesus' teaching that he can comfortably say that what separates the "blessed" from the "cursed" is the compassion they show to the destitute. The life of love, in other words, reveals those who have known the love of God. One is not saved by such a life, but such a life marks those who are saved. That is the theory, anyway.

Second, the Bible's insistence that God will condemn those who have oppressed or neglected the needy does not mean that the needy are automatically exempt from judgment. While care for the oppressed is a central criterion of judgment, so is reverence for the Creator. Presumably, the poor and oppressed can fail this latter criterion and so find themselves under judgment for reasons other than that described in Matthew 25. One Old Testament passage sets the sin of neglecting the Creator right alongside the sin of mistreating the oppressed (Jeremiah 2:26–37). In the New Testament, Romans 1:18–20 also underlines the point that refusing to honour the Creator merits divine judgment.

Within the Bible's logic—and, of course, you and I are at liberty to dismiss this reasoning—just as revering the Creator while neglecting our fellow creatures leaves us culpable, so does caring for creatures while ignoring the Creator. What Christ required of humanity was that they love thy neighbor and love thy Maker. His words are worth quoting:

> Hearing that Jesus had silenced the Sadducees, the Pharisees
> got together. One of them, an expert in the law, tested him
> with this question: "Teacher, which is the greatest command-
> ment in the Law?" Jesus replied: "Love the Lord your God
> with all your heart and with all your soul and with all your
> mind. This is the first and greatest commandment. And
> the second is like it: Love your neighbor as yourself. All the
> Law and the Prophets hang on these two commandments."
> (Matthew 22:34–40)

To put it bluntly, but no less accurately from a historical perspective,
Jesus would have condemned the philanthropic atheist with the
same "hell fire" gusto he directed at the religious hypocrite.

## REFLECTIONS

### The Church and the Needy

Throughout the ages the belief that the Messiah will "give decisions
for the poor of the earth" (Isaiah 11:4) has inspired innumerable
acts of charity within the church. In the early AD 30s the Jerusalem
church set up a large daily food roster for destitute widows (Acts
6:1–7). In the 40s and 50s the apostle Paul conducted what was
perhaps the world's first truly international aid project, collecting
money from the churches of Turkey, Greece, and Macedonia
for the famine-ravaged believers of Judaea (Romans 15:24–27;
1 Corinthians 16:1–4; 2 Corinthians 8–9). By AD 250 the church
in Rome was daily supporting fifteen hundred destitute men,
women, and children (Eusebius, *Ecclesiastical History* 6.43.11).

The influence of the ancient church's aid programs was so

great that the fourth-century pagan Emperor Julian (AD 331–62) wrote to his pagan priests insisting that pagan temples introduce a welfare system modelled on the Christian one: hostels for strangers, orphanages, and poverty-relief projects. He wanted to beat the Christians, or "Galileans" as he called them, at their own game. "For it is disgraceful," he complained to his high priest, "that, when no Jew ever has to beg [because of Jewish welfare], and the impious Galilaeans support not only their own poor but ours as well, all men see that our people lack aid from us" (Emperor Julian, "Letter 22, To Arcacius, High priest of Galatia." Vol. 2 of *The Works of the Emperor Julian*. Loeb Classical Library. Cambridge: Harvard University Press, 1999, 67–73). Emperor Julian died the following year, and his fear that the Christians might take over the empire through the stealth of their compassion was soon realised.

Things in the church have not always proceeded in this way. I include the above material not only to highlight the historical influence of the theme of Christ as Judge but also to remind fellow believers of a part of their heritage that is sometimes forgotten. While it is still true that most non-government welfare is conducted by church agencies (even in my post-Christian Australia), often this work is so centralised that the average Christian can easily forget about his or her obligation toward the needy or, worse, decide to leave such work to "headquarters."

## The Wealthy and the Needy

Contemporary Christians are not the only ones in the firing line, as it were, of Christ's pledge to bring justice for the needy. According to numerous studies, the wealthier a person is, the less generous they tend to be toward the poor. In 2016 the National

Australia Bank released its "Charitable Giving Index," which tracks the relative generosity of suburbs around the country. It revealed that Australia's most generous suburb—as a percentage of income given to charity—was the working class district of Castlemaine in the state of Victoria, a region with an average income in the second lowest quintile. By contrast, my own suburb (Roseville in New South Wales) is the twenty-first wealthiest postcode in the country—and in the top income quintile—but it is only the 299th most generous suburb. In short, those most favourable toward the poor tend to be the less affluent, and those least favourable toward the poor tend to be the most affluent.

More striking is the way my fellow Australians spend their money. The Australian Bureau of Statistics' *Household Expenditure Survey 2010* found that the average Australian household spends just $222 per year on charitable gifts. Compared with what we spend on other household items, this is embarrassing: $568 on our pets; $1,682 on alcoholic beverages; $2,729 on annual holidays; $3,248 on restaurant and takeaway meals. Wider society, no less than the church community, would do well to reflect afresh, and seriously, on the words of the future Judge:

> I was hungry and you gave me nothing to eat, I was thirsty and you gave me nothing to drink, I was a stranger and you did not invite me in, I needed clothes and you did not clothe me, I was sick and in prison and you did not look after me. (Matthew 25:42–43)

# 8

## FRIEND:

## THE SCANDAL OF HIS SOCIAL LIFE

**M**y introduction to the faith came not through family tradition or church attendance but through the irresistible power of friendship and good food. In Australia to this day, many government schools still have one lesson a week informally called "Scripture," where a volunteer from the local church, synagogue, mosque, or whatever will take students for thirty minutes and introduce them to the basics of their religion (parents just decide which "religion" they want their child to learn). My middle-aged Year 9 Scripture teacher had the courage one day to invite the entire class to her home for discussions about "God." The invitation would have gone unnoticed, except that she added: "I'll be making hamburgers, milkshakes, and scones." The menu topped the chocolate bars my friends and I were pinching from the local supermarket most days after school, so one Friday afternoon several weeks later we found ourselves sitting on a comfortable lounge in this woman's home with half-a-dozen other classmates feasting on her fantastic food and bracing ourselves for the god-bit.

As I looked around the room I was amazed that this woman would open her home (and kitchen) to us. Some of the lads there that day were noted "sinners" in our school: one was a drug user (and seller), one a class clown and bully, and another a petty thief with a string of break-and-enters to his credit. What was she thinking inviting us for a meal and discussion?

We returned the next Friday (with more hungry friends) and the next and the next. In fact, we turned up at this woman's house most Friday afternoons for the next year and a half. At no point was this teacher pushy or preachy. Her style was completely relaxed and incredibly generous. When her DVD player went missing one day—come to think of it, this was probably still the era of the video tape recorder—she made almost nothing of it, even though she suspected (reasonably enough) that one of us had taken it.

For me, her open, flexible, and generous attitude toward us "sinners" was the doorway into understanding the significance of Christ. As we ate and drank and talked, it was clear this was no mere missionary ploy on her part. She truly cared for us and treated us like friends or sons. Over the course of the next year she introduced me, as well as several others from the class, to the ultimate "Friend of Sinners," Jesus. Three of those boys are now pastors in churches. I visited her a few months ago. She was frail and unwell. But she was full of joy as we reminisced about her influence on me and my friends. She passed away shortly before I completed this manuscript. The book is dedicated to her memory.

My Scripture teacher embodied and illustrated for me one of the most striking dimensions of the ministry of the historical Jesus. Christ was famous in first-century Galilee for similar— though infinitely more significant—friendships with those classed "sinners."

## SINNERS AND ANCIENT PURITY RULES

"Sinners" were those in Jewish society who lived outside the laws of the Old Testament as interpreted by a Jewish faction known as Pharisees—perhaps from the Hebrew word *parush*, meaning "separated," i.e., separated from all things impure. Sinners were not necessarily prostitutes, murderers, and the like; they could just as easily be worldly businessmen who neglected synagogue attendance or conducted business with the occupying Romans (as the Jewish tax collectors did). Sinners were the immoral and irreligious in a broadly moral and religious society.

In the Judaism of Jesus' day, contact with sinners was strictly regulated (especially by the Pharisees). To enter the home of a sinner or to have a sinner enter your home was to become tainted by their "uncleanness." In order to become "clean" again, you would have to undergo a series of ritual washings. Even the house itself became "unclean" through the presence of a sinner. In the collection of ancient rabbinic rulings known as the Mishnah— still a holy book in Orthodox Judaism, as mentioned earlier—we learn what happens when tax collectors, thieves, or gentiles (i.e., non-Jews) enter your home:

> Concerning tax collectors who enter the house—the house is unclean. Concerning thieves who enter the house—only the place trodden by the feet of the thieves is unclean. And what do they render unclean? The foods, and the liquids, and the clay utensils which are open. But the couches and the seats and clay utensils which are sealed with a tight seal are clean. If there is a gentile with them, everything is unclean. (Mishnah Teharot 7:6)

Sharing meals with sinners (and gentiles) was especially objectionable. In ancient societies, eating and drinking were powerful symbols of human fellowship. To share food and drink with people was to identify with them and, in a sense, to endorse them. Professor Graham Stanton of Cambridge University puts it well:

> Sharing a meal with a friend today is often no more than a convenient way of consuming food. In the Graeco-Roman and Jewish world of the first century, however, eating food with another person was far more significant socially: it indicated that the invited person was being accepted into a relationship in which the bonds were as close as in family relations. One normally invited to meals only people whom one considered social and religious equals. ("Message and Miracles." *The Cambridge Companion to Jesus*. Edited by Markus Bockmeuhl. Cambridge: Cambridge University Press, 2001, 69.)

In a first-century Jewish setting, then, dining with sinners would be tantamount to endorsing their behaviour and so sharing their status.

## JESUS, THE FRIEND OF SINNERS

Jesus flouted these centuries-old customs. He regularly wined and dined with those considered moral and religious outcasts. He was so famous for this—"infamous" might be the better word—he was slandered in public about it. And the insult is preserved in our Christian texts. In a passage from Matthew's and Luke's shared source (known as Q) Jesus' detractors are quoted as saying:

Here is a glutton and a drunkard, a friend of tax collectors and sinners. (Luke 7:34, Matthew 11:19)

That such a rumour could have arisen about Jesus seems strange to many today, but it did. And historians regard these scandalous dining habits as one of the most striking features of Christ's public ministry. Consider the following examples from the Gospels:

While Jesus was having dinner at Levi's house, many tax collectors and sinners were eating with him and his disciples, for there were many who followed him. When the teachers of the law who were Pharisees saw him eating with the sinners and tax collectors, they asked his disciples: "Why does he eat with tax collectors and sinners?" (Mark 2:15–16)

Now the tax collectors and sinners were all gathering around to hear Jesus. But the Pharisees and the teachers of the law muttered, "This man welcomes sinners and eats with them.' (Luke 15:1–2)

Or take an incident in Jericho, 30 km northeast of Jerusalem, where Jesus is said to have spotted a chief tax collector and invited himself to the man's home:

[Jesus] said to him, "Zacchaeus, come down immediately. I must stay at your house today." So he came down at once and welcomed him gladly. All the people saw this and began to mutter, "He has gone to be the guest of a sinner." (Luke 19:5–7)

Of all the examples of this theme in Christ's life, it seems none is more poignant than one found in Luke 7. In first-century Galilee perhaps no one was considered more impure and deserving of divine judgment, in the opinion of first-century Jews, than a prostitute. And yet, on at least one occasion, while dining at the home of a Pharisee, Jesus welcomed to the table a woman euphemistically introduced to us as having "lived a sinful life in that town":

> A woman in that town who lived a sinful life learned that Jesus was eating at the Pharisee's house, so she came there with an alabaster jar of perfume. As she stood behind him at his feet weeping, she began to wet his feet with her tears. Then she wiped them with her hair, kissed them and poured perfume on them. When the Pharisee who had invited him saw this, he said to himself, "If this man were a prophet, he would know who is touching him and what kind of woman she is—that she is a sinner." (Luke 7:37–39)

The woman had heard Jesus was in town and in her desperation to meet him she gate-crashed the home of a Pharisee—thus rendering the Pharisee's home unclean according to custom. Much to the displeasure of the Pharisee and the other guests, Jesus let this woman touch him as she wept at his feet hopeful of God's mercy. The touch itself would have rendered Jesus unclean in the eyes of many. "If this man were a prophet," thought the Pharisee, "he would know who is touching him and what kind of woman she is—that she is a sinner."

Ironically, Jesus not only knew that the woman was a sinner, he knew what his host was thinking and responded by telling him a delightful, if somewhat unrealistic, hypothetical story about a bank manager with two clients. One owed him the equivalent of $50,000, the other $5,000. Both debts were cancelled freely. "Which of them will love [the moneylender] more?" asks Jesus. Let me continue the quotation from Luke 7:

> Jesus answered him, "Simon, I have something to tell you." "Tell me, teacher," he said. "Two people owed money to a certain moneylender. One owed him five hundred denarii, and the other fifty. Neither of them had the money to pay him back, so he forgave the debts of both. Now which of them will love him more?" Simon replied, "I suppose the one who had the bigger debt forgiven." "You have judged correctly," Jesus said. Then he turned toward the woman and said to Simon, "Do you see this woman? I came into your house. You did not give me any water for my feet, but she wet my feet with her tears and wiped them with her hair. You did not give me a kiss, but this woman, from the time I entered, has not stopped kissing my feet. You did not put oil on my head, but she has poured perfume on my feet. Therefore, I tell you, her many sins have been forgiven—as her great love has shown. But whoever has been forgiven little loves little." (Luke 7:40–47)

The woman's extravagant act of devotion reveals her love for Jesus as the (hoped-for) source of divine forgiveness. Perhaps she had heard the rumours about this man who bypassed the temple priests and offered mercy to sinners directly and freely. Perhaps she had even heard Jesus preach, as she stood at the back of the crowd.

Whatever drove her to seek out Jesus, she received the words she longed to hear, words I should think many would want to hear:

> Then Jesus said to her, "Your sins are forgiven." The other guests began to say among themselves, "Who is this who even forgives sins?" Jesus said to the woman, "Your faith has saved you; go in peace." (Luke 7:48–50)

In light of an incident like this, it is no wonder that Jesus' contemporaries—especially the religious leaders—slandered him as the "friend of sinners," a tag Jesus perhaps took as a compliment.

---

**BOOK NOTES** | An excellent scholarly survey of the theme of Jesus' scandalous dining habits is Craig Blomberg, *Contagious Holiness: Jesus' Meals with Sinners*. Downers Grove, IL: InterVarsity Press, 2005.

---

## JUDGE AND FRIEND: THE PARADOX OF JESUS' LIFE

We are left with a paradox in the life of Jesus. The man who regularly proclaimed the coming judgment befriended those one might have thought were first in line for divine displeasure. The Judge of sinners was also the Friend of sinners.

According to the Gospels and the wider New Testament, this paradox was resolved in the death and resurrection of Jesus (studied in chapters 9 and 10 below). Through these, Christ is said to have borne divine judgment for all who accept his hand of friendship.

Jesus' openness toward sinners, then, was a deliberate sign of the welcoming grace of God. His preaching declared that grace, his suffering secured grace, and his scandalous social life embodied grace in a tangible way. Through his meals with the undeserving, he sought to demonstrate the friendship with sinners he believed God so keenly desires.

## REFLECTIONS

Let me unpack some of the ways that Christian thought has, with varying degrees of success, appropriated this historical dimension of Christ's life.

### "Left" and "Right" in Early Christianity

Jesus' fraternising with sinners heavily influenced the social conduct of the early church. Historians note that the first Christians overturned the social distinctions and attendant discrimination between Jew and gentile, pure and impure, saint and sinner.

It was not that these disciples were all "lefty relativists." Far from it! Unlike modern society (and frequently modern Christendom), the ancient church was both right wing and left wing at the same time. The ever-widening divide in modern social discourse between left and right is one of the intellectual blind spots of our culture. The first Christians were utterly devoted to Jesus' ethical standards, which included clear guidelines on marriage, sex, honesty, and so on, and, at the same time, utterly devoted to the social generosity Jesus had embodied. They ate with gentiles and the immoral, they insisted that the rich among them should give honour (and assistance) to their poor brothers and sisters, they gladly accepted the shame of aligning themselves with people who were weak, sick, and imprisoned, and their treatment of women—despite much bad press today on this issue—was enlightened.

The famous judgment of Rodney Stark, former professor of sociology at University of Washington, now at Baylor University, captures the appeal of the early church well:

> Therefore, as I conclude this study, I find it necessary to confront what appears to me to be the ultimate factor in the rise of Christianity. . . . The simple phrase "For God so loved the world . . ." would have puzzled an educated pagan. And the notion that the gods care how we treat one another would have been dismissed as patently absurd. . . . This was the moral climate in which Christianity taught that mercy is one of the primary virtues—that a merciful God requires humans to be merciful. . . . This was revolutionary stuff. Indeed, it was the cultural basis for the revitalization of the Roman world groaning under a host of miseries. . . . In my judgment, a major way in which Christianity served as a revitalization movement within the empire was in offering a coherent culture that was entirely stripped of ethnicity. All were welcome without need to dispense with ethnic ties. . . . Christianity also prompted liberating social relations between the sexes and within the family . . . [and] greatly modulated class differences—more than rhetoric was involved when slave and noble greeted one another as brothers in Christ. Finally, what Christianity gave to its converts was nothing less than their humanity. In this sense virtue was its own reward. (*The Rise of Christianity*. New York: HarperCollins, 1997, 209–15.)

None of this would have emerged within the ancient church if they had not been powerfully aware that their Teacher, Judge, and Messiah was also a Friend to those normally excluded from society on moral and religious grounds.

## Being a Friend of Sinners

When I was first learning about Christ, as a 15–16 year old, I had no difficulty believing that God and Christians cared for me. This was so even though I knew I had not exactly lived the Christian life. The reason was that the main Christian in my life was the Scripture teacher I mentioned earlier, and she was the embodiment of a "friend of sinners."

When I visited my old teacher recently in the hospital, I reminded her of a particularly striking example of her friend-of-sinners approach to us all those years ago. (Actually, she remembered it all too well.) On one occasion after a late-night school party, one of my friends, David (not his real name), was heavily drunk. Amid episodes of vomiting he begged us not to take him home, fearful of his military father's reaction. One in our group came up with an idea, and I am embarrassed now as I recall it: "Hey, doesn't the Scripture teacher live just down the road?"

Ten minutes later we were knocking on this woman's door, interrupting her own dinner party. The fact that we all thought this was a perfectly reasonable idea at the time tells you what kind of person she seemed to us. The fact that she did not bat an eyelid tells you even more; and she was a strict teetotaler! She showed us in, let us throw David in the shower, and provided him with some of her son's old clothes. Then she let us put him in one of the spare bedrooms for the night as she went back to her guests.

When we came to collect him the next morning about 10 a.m., there was the Scripture teacher cooking breakfast for David—not that he much felt like it!

When you have that kind of Christian in your life, coming to believe that Christ and the church love sinners is easy. Of course, I later learnt why many doubt the divine love and doubt the love of the church, but that was only after mixing with some moralising Christians for a while. In those early days, I had no idea one could be *bigoted* and *Christian* at the same time.

My point is a simple one, and it has been borne out (and sometimes forgotten) time and again in the history of Christianity: those who know the Friend of Sinners will be a friend to sinners.

# 9

# TEMPLE:
## THE RELOCATION OF GOD'S PRESENCE

There used to be a large sign on the northern side of the town of Cooma near the Australian snow fields (yes, there is some snow in Australia, sometimes) which read: "Cooma: Gateway to the Snowy Mountains." I remember the excitement I felt as a child passing through Cooma on the way to our annual holiday in the Snowy Mountains. My entire body would tingle with expectation as I wound down the window and felt the chilled mountain air streaming across my face. It is one of my most potent early childhood memories. And I still can't resist sticking my head out of the window as I pass through Cooma to this day!

This childhood sense of anticipation, however, is nothing compared to the excitement of ancient Jews as they streamed toward Jerusalem for the annual Passover festival and arrived at the town of Bethphage—"gateway to the holy city"—just under a couple of kilometres from Jerusalem. Once pilgrims made their way up the road from Bethphage to the top of the Mount of Olives, they would be greeted by a magnificent panoramic view of the holy city, just a few hundred metres or so away. At the front of their view was the huge Jerusalem temple, a site approximately the size of today's largest football stadiums.

The temple was the centre of Israel's national and religious life. This was where God chose to dwell, according to the Hebrew Scriptures; it was where sacrifices for the forgiveness of sins could be made; it was where the country's leading teachers could be heard in the vast temple courts; it was where pilgrims gathered in tens of thousands, especially at Passover time, to sing and pray to the one true God. For the devout Jew, arriving at the crest of the Mount of Olives and looking down at the temple of God must have stirred up extraordinary feelings of national pride and spiritual awe.

## THE DONKEY AND THE KING

In the midst of this already heightened sense of occasion, toward the end of his public career as a teacher and healer, Jesus paused and told his disciples to do something that sounded suspiciously like the fulfilment of an Old Testament prophecy about the anointed descendant of King David. In the book of Zechariah (written around 500 years earlier) the prophet predicted that the long-awaited king would arrive in Jerusalem riding on a donkey:

> Rejoice greatly, Daughter Zion! Shout, Daughter Jerusalem!
> See, your king comes to you, righteous and victorious, lowly
> and riding on a donkey, on a colt, the foal of a donkey. . . .
> He will proclaim peace to the nations. His rule will extend
> from sea to sea and from the River to the ends of the earth.
> (Zechariah 9:9–10)

According to the Gospels, Jesus arranged to enter Jerusalem in April AD 30 mounted—you guessed it—on a donkey. To quote Matthew's version of the incident (which, like Luke's, is derived from the Gospel of Mark):

> As they approached Jerusalem and came to Bethphage on the Mount of Olives, Jesus sent two disciples, saying to them, "Go to the village ahead of you, and at once you will find a donkey tied there, with her colt by her. Untie them and bring them to me. If anyone says anything to you, say that the Lord needs them, and he will send them right away."
>
> The disciples went and did as Jesus had instructed them. They brought the donkey and the colt and placed their cloaks on them for Jesus to sit on. A very large crowd spread their cloaks on the road, while others cut branches from the trees and spread them on the road. The crowds that went ahead of him and those that followed shouted, "Hosanna to the Son of David!" "Blessed is he who comes in the name of the Lord!" "Hosanna in the highest heaven!" (Matthew 21:1–3, 6–9)

The Zechariah prophecy just quoted was so well known that the disciples must have been bursting with excitement at the thought that finally, after being so coy about his status, Jesus was doing something *overtly* royal. The excitement spilled over into the crowd of pilgrims as they lay down cloaks and tree branches, the ancient equivalent of the red carpet, and began shouting in unison, "Hosanna to the Son of David!" The word Hosanna literally means "Lord, save us!" When combined with a reference to the descendant of King David, the expression carried powerful overtones about the arrival of a kingdom that would, according to the prophecy of Zechariah, "extend from sea to sea and from the River to the ends of the earth."

What the Gospels describe, then, is not a simple "three cheers for Jesus." This was a significant public parade acclaiming the man from Nazareth as the heir of the coming kingdom of God. For the first time, Jesus' authority as the messianic king was enthusiastically and publicly embraced. The king has arrived at the temple of God. It must have been spine-tingling stuff.

## JESUS VERSUS THE TEMPLE

But, as so often in Christ's life, Jesus reinterpreted this grand expectation in an unexpected way. The text from Matthew (like that of Luke and Mark) continues with Jesus' dramatic entry into the Jerusalem temple:

> Jesus entered the temple courts and drove out all who were buying and selling there. He overturned the tables of the money changers and the benches of those selling doves. "It is written," he said to them, "'My house will be called a house of prayer,' but you are making it 'a den of robbers.'" (Matthew 21:12–13)

According to the Gospels, Jesus did several unexpected, almost foolhardy, things in his encounter with the temple authorities, any one of which could have landed him in prison. Like a modern stadium, the temple had paid security.

In the first place, Jesus drove out those who were buying and selling. At Passover time families were required to make individual sacrifices of various animals. Rather than bring their own stock from home, pilgrims could purchase sacrificial animals on site. This began as a service but was very easily abused. When you are at a football stadium without any food or drink, you end up paying $8 for a bottle of water and $15 for a sandwich. When you were in Jerusalem at Passover time without a sacrificial animal, you were at the mercy of the priestly price. This so outraged Jesus that he drove them all out, made them pack up their stalls and leave the temple courts. How he pulled this off, we are not told. The main court of the temple where all these transactions took place was about 150 metres long and 300 metres wide, and it would have been filled with pilgrims.

Second, Jesus overturned the tables of the moneychangers. These were temple accountants in charge of currency exchange. In this period all adult Jewish males had to pay an annual temple tax, handed over just before Passover. Temple officials, however, accepted only one currency, silver shekels of Tyre. So, before pilgrims could pay their dues they had to change their coins. And, of course, there was a fee for the exchange. This too was open to abuse, and Jesus was appalled. Imagine the scene described above: tables overturned one by one, coins rolling across the temple court and crowds of the Jewish faithful standing around gob-smacked at the teacher from Nazareth.

## HISTORY NOTE

The annual temple tax was one half-shekel, or the equivalent of a denarius—perhaps about US $100 in modern terms. The silver content of shekels produced in Tyre and Jerusalem, however, was generally higher than that of Roman denarii (90 percent and 80 percent respectively), so the temple officials ruled that only Tyrian silver was acceptable for the annual tax. This decision was probably as much concerned with the issue of "purity" as "economy" but, as so often in religion, the two frequently coalesce.

Jesus also overturned "the benches of those selling doves." We might have thought the previous reference to "those who were buying and selling" would have included those who sold doves. But these priestly salesmen are marked out for special attention in the Gospels. Why? Doves were sold to people who could not afford the usual sacrificial animals. The Old Testament text of Leviticus 5:7 stipulates: "Anyone who cannot afford a lamb is to bring two doves." Dove-sellers, then, were profiteering at the expense of the poor, and doing so in the name of religion. Given Christ's teaching about the obligation to care for the needy, it is no wonder his feelings reached this climax. He overturned, we are told, not just the dove-sellers' tables, but also their seats. In a very real sense, Jesus' actions against the temple were an expression of the messianic mission foretold in the Old Testament book of Isaiah (discussed in chapter 5): "with righteousness he will judge the needy, with justice he will give decisions for the poor of the earth."

Once Jesus had everyone's attention in this massive courtyard, he launched into a speech based on an Old Testament text (Isaiah 56:7): "My house will be called a house of prayer," Jesus said, "But you are making it a 'den of robbers.'" These few words—which are just a summary of what he said—make it perfectly clear that Jesus believed the temple had become corrupt. There were more than fifteen thousand priests in Israel associated with the temple in this period, and Jesus had just described them as a pack of thieves.

It is difficult to convey just how explosive all this must have been. Jesus has not simply interrupted a church service to offer a thought-for-the-day. He has first gone public with his status as the promised anointed king and then denounced the central feature of Israel's national and spiritual life—its glorious temple.

## JESUS AS THE TEMPLE

It is hardly surprising that Jesus would be dead by the end of the week. It is also not surprising that one of the central charges laid against him at his trial was his reported contempt for the temple. Matthew's Gospel records:

> Finally two came forward and declared, "This fellow said, 'I am able to destroy the temple of God and rebuild it in three days.'" Then the high priest stood up and said to Jesus, "Are you not going to answer?" (Matthew 26:60–62)

Jesus did not answer this charge, perhaps because he did actually say something like this, even if he meant it in a symbolic way. Historically revealing is the fact that in the Gospel of John's account of the clearing of the temple (probably written independently of the other three Gospels) we hear a statement from Jesus that comes very close to the one recalled at his trial:

> The Jews then responded to him, "What sign can you show us
> to prove your authority to do all this?" Jesus answered them,
> "Destroy this temple, and I will raise it again in three days."
> They replied, "It has taken forty-six years to build this temple,
> and you are going to raise it in three days?" But the temple he
> had spoken of was his body. After he was raised from the dead,
> his disciples recalled what he had said. Then they believed the
> scripture and the words that Jesus had spoken. (John 2:18–22)

At first sight, this is a bizarre statement: Jesus' body, crucified
and raised, is the temple! However, this is not the first time Jesus has
identified himself with the temple. The theme emerges a number
of times in the Gospels. We get hints of it every time Jesus hands
out divine forgiveness to people. In first-century Judaism, only the
temple priests could pronounce forgiveness and, even then, only
after the appropriate sacrifice had been offered. This is why, after
Jesus forgave the prostitute at the home of Simon the Pharisee, as
discussed in the previous chapter, the guests murmured, "Who
is this who even forgives sins?" (Luke 7:49b). Jesus handed out
forgiveness whenever anyone humbly approached *him*. He acted
like a mobile temple.

An explicit comparison between Jesus and the temple is found
in Matthew 12 in a scene set long before Jesus took on the temple
priests. The Pharisees had criticised Jesus' disciples for doing what
looked like work on the Sabbath day. Jesus responded:

> Haven't you read what David did when he and his companions
> were hungry? He entered the house of God, and he and his
> companions ate the consecrated bread—which was not lawful

for them to do, but only for the priests. Or haven't you read in the Law that the priests on Sabbath duty in the temple desecrate the Sabbath day [i.e., do work on the Sabbath] and yet are innocent? I tell you that something greater than the temple is here. (Matthew 12:3–6)

The logic goes like this: priests are exempt from the Sabbath law when working within the precinct of the temple; how much more then are the disciples exempt when working in the vicinity of the Messiah. Jesus, according to these words, is *more* than the temple. This is an extraordinary statement in its first-century context. Commenting on this theme, the British New Testament scholar N. T. Wright, now Research Professor at the University of St. Andrews in Scotland, remarks:

Jesus' actions during the last week of his life focused on the Temple. Judaism had two great incarnational symbols: Temple and Torah. Jesus seems to have believed it was his vocation to upstage the one and outflank the other. Judaism spoke of the presence of her God in her midst, in the pillar of cloud and fire, in the Presence ("Shekinah") in the Temple. Jesus acted and spoke as if he thought he were a one-man counter-Temple movement. (N. T. Wright, *The Challenge of Jesus.* Downers Grove, IL: InterVarsity Press, 1999, 113–14.)

## REFLECTIONS

When Jesus rode into Jerusalem, entered the temple, and declared its ministry bankrupt, he was not acting as a mere religious radical.

According to the witness of the Gospel writers, he was acting as God's replacement temple or, perhaps more accurately, as the reality to which the temple pointed all along. All that the temple had meant for Israel for almost one thousand years was now to be found in Israel's Messiah. The presence of God that human beings so longed for was to be found through a personal connection with Christ, not in a building in East Jerusalem. The hunger for divine teaching could be satisfied, not in the courts of a glorious sanctuary but by feeding on the words of Jesus. True "pilgrims" could henceforth declare their praises, not within the walls of one sacred building but wherever people gathered in honour of the Messiah. And forgiveness of sins could be enjoyed through the one priestly sacrifice of Jesus, not through priest and sacrifice.

It is no wonder that as Jesus breathed his last breath on the cross, just a week after his daring confrontation with the temple authorities, the inner sanctum of the temple itself was disturbed. As Matthew (following Mark) tells us:

> And when Jesus had cried out again in a loud voice, he gave up his spirit. At that moment the curtain of the temple was torn in two from top to bottom. (Matthew 27:50–51)

The Jerusalem temple was eventually destroyed some forty years after Jesus' death, when in August AD 70 Roman troops stormed Jerusalem to end a bitter five-year rebellion. Of the few remains of the temple is a 50-or-so-metre-long section of the western wall, called the Wailing Wall. Modern Jews congregate there to this day to cry out to God for the promised messiah and for the restoration of God's holy sanctuary. Unfortunately (from the Jewish point of view), standing where the temple once stood is the Dome of the Rock, the oldest existing Islamic monument in the world, built around AD 690. This spot is the world's most hotly disputed piece of real estate. And yet, Orthodox Jews maintain their doctrines and hopes about the spot. A sign remains there to this day alerting passersby to the significance of the site. It reads:

> The temple mount is the focal point of Creation. In the center of the mountain lies the "Foundation Stone" of the world. Jews have prayed in its shadow for hundreds of years, an expression of their faith in the rebuilding of the Temple. The Sages said about it: "The Divine Presence never moves from the Western Wall."

From the point of view of the first followers of Jesus, the temple was really overthrown and replaced in April AD 30. From the time of Christ's death and resurrection, said the early Christians, a new temple was established for all nations. All who want to locate the Creator's presence, learn his teaching, and enjoy his forgiveness can do so simply by embracing the Messiah, the new temple.

# 10

## SAVIOUR:
### THE MEANING OF HIS DEATH

The Gospels provide many fascinating portraits of Jesus—as teacher, healer, judge, and so on—but I would give them all away just to know him as Saviour.

## THE CLICHÉ OF SALVATION

Because "salvation" is so central to the Christian faith, it is a theme prone to being seen as an embarrassing cliché. "Are you saved?" now seems like the question of the televangelist, not a grown-up, modern spirituality. Even long-term believers feel awkward with this salvation language. For the skeptical it is just funny, even ridiculous.

But things only become clichés when an originally sound idea gets overused and misused. It's important, then, to strip back the regrettable accumulations and look again at the original.

The early history of Australia's convict colony was not quite the godless wasteland some imagine. And one remarkable incident underlines perfectly why the theme of Jesus as Saviour is far more than an uncomfortable piece of religious jargon.

# THE CONVICT AND THE SAVIOUR

At fifteen years of age Samuel Peyton was sentenced to "seven years" for the "theft of a piece of cloth"—a frightening thought when I recall what I was getting up to at fifteen. Luckily, he was pardoned after just two years in prison. He would not be so lucky the second time around.

A couple of years later Peyton was caught in possession of a stolen watch, which he claimed he won in a card game. The explanation did not wash and he was sentenced to "seven years transportation." In May 1787 Samuel Peyton was bound for Sydney with 774 other convicts, chained in the hull of the *Alexander*, in what is called the "First Fleet," the European beginnings of Australia.

On arriving at Sydney Cove eight months later, Peyton was set to work as a stone mason supporting the flurry of early colonial building activity—the hospital, the prison, and, of course, the governor's house. Within five months the young Peyton was again in trouble. This time he was found in an officer's quarters trying to steal, so the report states, a "shirt, stockings and a comb." One gets the impression Samuel was more foolhardy than evil.

Peyton was promptly tried and sentenced on Monday, June 23, 1788, and on Wednesday the 25th he was hanged on Sydney's public gallows, where the exclusive harbourside Four Seasons Hotel now stands. He was just 21 years old. (I wish to thank the NSW State Archives—and my wife, Buff—for helping me uncover and verify the details of Peyton's all-too-short life.)

Samuel Peyton would be just another name in a convict log

were it not for a letter he wrote to his mother, with the assistance of an unnamed friend, the night before his hanging. One of the First Fleet officers, Watkin Tench, was so taken with the letter that he copied it out in his own journal, which was later published. Officer Tench was interested only in highlighting for his readership back in England "that not the ignorant and untaught only have provoked the justice of their country to banish them to this remote region." For me, though, Peyton's letter illustrates one of the most enduring legacies of the Gospels' portrait of Jesus. From the first century to the eighteenth and beyond, people around the world have found in Christ a Saviour. Peyton's letter reads:

My dear mother! with what agony of soul do I dedicate the few last moments of my life to bid you an eternal adieu: my doom being irrevocably fixed, and ere this hour tomorrow I shall have entered into an unknown and endless eternity. I will not distress your tender maternal feelings by any long comment on the cause of my present misfortune.

Let it therefore suffice to say that impelled by that strong propensity to evil, which neither the virtuous precepts nor example of the best of parents could eradicate, I have at length fallen an unhappy, though just, victim to my own follies. Too late I regret my inattention to your admonitions, and feel myself sensibly affected by the remembrance of the many anxious moments you have passed on my account.

For these and all my other transgressions, however great, I supplicate the Divine forgiveness; and encouraged by the promises of that Saviour who died for us all, I trust to receive that mercy in the world to come, which my offences have deprived me of in this.

The affliction which this will cost you, I hope the Almighty will enable you to bear. Banish from your memory all my former indiscretions, and let the cheering hope of a happy meeting hereafter console you for my loss. Sincerely penitent for my sins; sensible of the justice of my conviction and sentence, and firmly relying on the merits of a Blessed Redeemer, I trust I shall yet experience that peace which this world cannot give.

Commend my soul to Divine mercy. I bid you an eternal farewell.

> Your unhappy dying son,
> Samuel Peyton,
> Sydney Cove, Port Jackson,
> New South Wales, 24th June 1788

(Tench's diary was recently reprinted as *Watkin Tench 1788: Edited and Introduced by Tim Flannery*. Melbourne: Text Publishing Company, 1996. Peyton's letter is quoted on pages 68–69.)

Peyton's letter captures perfectly a theme of Christ's life that appears across the range of our earliest sources. To quote Peyton, Jesus is the "Saviour who died for us all."

## HISTORY NOTE

The saviour theme emerges strongly in L, the letters of Paul, and the Gospel of Mark. Matthew and Luke (who used Mark's Gospel as a source) both endorse and expand the saviour theme found in Mark. Matthew's and Luke's shared source, Q, does not emphasise Jesus' role as saviour. This is partly explained by the fact that Q was not a narrative portrait of Jesus but principally a collection of his sayings.

## SAVIOUR IN LIFE

In chapter 5 we explored the meaning of Jesus' "surname"— which, you will remember, was not a surname at all. "Christ" (or in Anglicised Hebrew, "Messiah") is a title for the one "anointed" to speak and act on God's behalf. But the Gospel writers gave another, equally important, title to Jesus. In fact, the two titles appear alongside each other in a passage usually associated with Christmastime:

> I bring you good news that will cause great joy for all the people. Today in the town of David a Savior has been born to you; he is the Messiah, the Lord. (Luke 2:10–11)

If the title "Messiah" or "Christ" captured Jesus' status as the one endowed with divine authority, the title "Saviour" captured Jesus' mission to rescue people from divine judgment.

## HISTORY NOTE

A very early creedal statement about Jesus as saviour from judgment appears in one of Paul's first extant letters: "You turned to God from idols to serve the living and true God, and to wait for his Son from heaven, whom he raised from the dead—Jesus, who rescues us from the coming wrath" (1 Thessalonians 1:9–10).

Even Jesus' given name conveyed this theme. "Jesus," which is an Anglicised form of the Hebrew name *Yeshua*, comes from the verb "to save." While in the modern world most of us are unaware of the meaning of our names, in antiquity, and especially in ancient Judaism, given names were transparent in meaning and highly significant. The Gospel of Matthew makes the point explicit:

> She will give birth to a son, and you are to give him the name Jesus, because he will save his people from their sins.
> (Matthew 1:21)

My point is simple. According to the Gospels, by name as well as by title Jesus is the one who came to save men and women from divine judgment.

Here we arrive at one of the striking differences between the first century and the twenty-first. Jesus lived in a culture so keenly aware of God's just judgment that he had difficulty convincing people that "sinners" could be welcomed to the divine table. Ironically, probably under the influence of Jesus' teaching, many in the West today are so used to the notion of divine love that Christ would now have difficulty convincing us we were sinners in the first place.

But Jesus never taught that God accepts men and women because he is pleased with the way they are. Far from it. He insisted that humanity's incessant search for wealth at the expense of the poor is truly damnable (Matthew 25:31–46; Luke 16:19–31). He said that a person's love for the things of creation while ignoring the Creator himself is what makes him or her a sinner. This is a point made clear in the famous Parable of the Prodigal Son (Luke 15:11–32). There, in a metaphor about the sinner, Jesus tells how a young son (the sinner) offended his father (God) by demanding the family inheritance and then leaving home to spend his father's goods on himself. The son wanted everything the father had to offer; he just did not want the father himself. That is what a sinner is, according to Jesus.

And it is only against this backdrop that his title "Saviour" can be understood. According to the Gospels, Jesus perceived his entire mission in terms of saving sinners from the coming judgment.

As we saw in chapter 7, Jesus sought out those one might have thought were first in line for judgment, and he offered them mercy. To the "sinful woman" who came to him in the Pharisee's house he declared, "Your faith has saved you; go in peace" (Luke 7:50). To offer another potent example, as Jesus neared Jerusalem for his final week, he spotted a wealthy tax collector named Zacchaeus, someone who had been milking fellow Jews on behalf of the local powers and creaming a fat profit off the top for himself. According to the Gospel of Luke, Jesus invited himself to the man's home— much to the consternation of the religious authorities—and made a statement that could easily stand as a banner over his entire mission:

Jesus said to him, "Today salvation has come to this house, because this man, too, is a son of Abraham. For the Son of Man came to seek and to save the lost." (Luke 19:9–10)

## THE SAVIOUR AND HIS SUPPER

The saviour theme reaches its climax in the final hours of Jesus' life, in his Last Supper and death on a cross. I stated in the previous chapter that Jesus arrived in Jerusalem during Passover week. At this time Jews from all over the Roman world made their pilgrimage to the holy city to take part in this most sacred day of the Jewish calendar. They were there to commemorate Israel's liberation from Egyptian slavery more than a millennium before. A lamb would be sacrificed to recall the original Passover lamb whose blood was placed on the doorframes of Jewish homes. When God came in anger against the Egyptians that fateful night centuries earlier, he saw the blood of the lamb, says the Old Testament book of Exodus, and preserved the Hebrew families (you can read the story in Exodus 12). His judgment *fell upon* Egypt but *passed over* the people of Israel. The Passover festival was a commemoration, in other words, of God saving his people. This is still its meaning among modern Jews.

Jesus managed to avoid arrest for most of Passover week. His days were spent speaking to large crowds of pilgrims in the temple courtyard, before slipping away at night to a friend's home a few kilometres east of Jerusalem. The final night was different. It was Passover Eve and Jesus wanted to celebrate this special occasion with his colleagues in the holy city itself.

When Jesus sat down to celebrate the Passover meal of April AD

30, things would have proceeded in much the same way as they had for the twelve hundred years before (and the two thousand years since): cooked lamb, traditional spices, wine, unleavened bread, prayers, songs, and so on. But Jesus added one highly unusual element that evening. He took the bread and wine in his hands and gave them an intriguing new meaning:

> Jesus took bread, and when he had given thanks, he broke it and gave it to his disciples, saying, "Take and eat; this is my body." Then he took a cup, and when he had given thanks, he gave it to them, saying, "Drink from it, all of you. This is my blood of the covenant, which is poured out for many for the forgiveness of sins." (Matthew 26:26–28)

Jesus took the traditional Passover themes of "blood" and "forgiveness" and related them to what is about to happen to him. Jesus' blood, just like that of the Passover lamb, would be poured out for the forgiveness of God's people. God's judgment would fall upon the "lamb" (Jesus) so that it might pass over "sinners." This, according to Jesus, was his destiny. This was how the undeserving could be welcomed into his kingdom. This was how he would be the Saviour.

Within hours of this Last Supper, Jesus was arrested, put on trial, and found guilty of "blasphemy" and "crimes against the temple." However, at this time, Israel was an occupied territory. The Jewish leadership (mainly the priestly Sadducees) did not have the authority to administer the death penalty. That power lay with the Roman Prefect, Pontius Pilate, who saw in Jesus' claim to be Messiah a treasonous challenge to the authority of the Roman Emperor Tiberius. In socio-political terms, then, it was the Romans who killed Jesus. But political explanations are only one way of looking at the event. The Gospels insist that the truest meaning of Jesus' death is found not in politics but in the Messiah's own explanation. Jesus died as a Saviour, the lamb for a worldwide "Passover."

## THE SAVIOUR AND HIS CROSS

Given the prominence of the "saving" theme in the Gospels, it is no wonder that, when Jesus is eventually tried and sentenced to death, the claim to be able to save people would be turned around as an insult. What kind of "Saviour," reasoned his detractors, is unable to save himself? Luke's Gospel records how Jesus was mocked at the site of his crucifixion, just 100 metres beyond Jerusalem's walls:

> The people stood watching [the crucifixion], and the rulers even sneered at him. They said, "He saved others; let him save himself if he is God's Messiah, the Chosen One." The soldiers also came up and mocked him. They offered him wine vinegar and said, "If you are the king of the Jews, save yourself." There was a written notice above him, which read: THIS IS THE KING OF THE JEWS. One of the criminals who hung there hurled insults at him: "Aren't you the Messiah? Save yourself and us!" (Luke 23:35–39)

First the religious rulers, then the Roman soldiers, then one of the criminals crucified alongside Jesus, all draw attention to the irony of the situation. The one who claimed to *save* people from the coming judgment could not even *save* himself from the wrath of Rome.

As an historical aside, the ancient world interpreted Christ's crucifixion to be proof of the folly of Christianity. What kind of Saviour ends up naked on a Roman cross? As the apostle Paul lamented, "the message of the cross is foolishness" in the eyes of the world (1 Corinthians 1:18). This very perspective can be detected in the criticisms of Christ and Christianity found in the Roman writer Tacitus, the Jewish Talmud, and the Greek satirist Lucian who dismisses the "saviour" of the Christians as "that crucified sophist."

It must be remembered that the ancients regarded crucifixion as the most shameful of deaths. Of the three main methods of execution—decapitation, burning, and crucifixion—crucifixion was considered the most severe, and Roman citizens were officially exempt from ever undergoing it. The Roman writer and statesman, Cicero (106–43 BC), described crucifixion as the *summum supplicium*, the "supreme punishment" (Cicero, *The Verrine Orations, Volume II, Against Verres, Part 2.* Translated by L. H. G. Greenwood. Loeb Classical Library, 293. Cambridge: Harvard University Press, 1935, 2.168). A century later the Roman philosopher Seneca (4 BC–AD 65) described the fate of crucifixion in the following way:

> Can anyone be found who would prefer wasting away in pain dying limb by limb, or letting out his life drop by drop, rather than expiring once for all? Can any man be found willing to be fastened to the accursed tree, long sickly, already

deformed, swelling with ugly tumors on shoulders and chest, and drawing the breath of life amid long-drawn-out agony? He would have many excuses for dying even before mounting the cross. (Seneca, *Epistles*. Translated by Richard M. Gummere. Loeb Classical Library, 77. Cambridge: Harvard University Press, 1925, 101.14.)

| | |
|---|---|
| The still-standard work on ancient crucifixion and its relevance to Christianity was written forty years ago by the great University of Tübingen Professor Martin Hengel, *Crucifixion in the Ancient World and the Folly of the Message of the Cross*, Philadelphia: Fortress, 1977. | **BOOK NOTES** |

One can see in such texts the very real dilemma faced by the first Christians as they tried to convince the Roman world that a crucified man was the Lord and Saviour of the world. The fact that they pulled it off is an even greater historical puzzle, but one beyond the scope of this book.

What many saw as a shameful failure, paradoxically, was viewed as a beautiful victory by those who really knew what Jesus taught. It was precisely in not saving himself from the cross that Jesus became the Saviour of the world. In a twist of outcomes that can be seen only through the lens of Jesus' teaching, sinners could be saved from God's judgment only because the Saviour bore that judgment himself.

According to Luke's Gospel, at least one person present when Christ was crucified spotted this paradox. Hearing the mockery of the leaders, soldiers, and the criminal, a second criminal, himself facing the *summum supplicium*, rebuked the first and turned to Jesus as Saviour:

> But the other criminal rebuked him [the first criminal]. "Don't you fear God," he said, "since you are under the same sentence? We are punished justly, for we are getting what our deeds deserve. But this man has done nothing wrong." Then he said, "Jesus, remember me when you come into your kingdom." Jesus answered him, "Truly I tell you, today you will be with me in paradise." It was now about noon, and darkness came over the whole land until three in the afternoon, for the sun stopped shining. And the curtain of the temple was torn in two. Jesus called out with a loud voice, "Father, into your hands I commit my spirit." When he had said this, he breathed his last. (Luke 23:40–46)

For as long as I have known the Gospels I have loved these words. There is no religion here, no complex theology, just a simple admission of unworthiness and a daring, though insightful, request for mercy. One struggles to think how anyone could have believed in that moment that Jesus possessed a "kingdom"—he certainly would not have looked very royal at that time. However he worked it out, this criminal saw what others missed: not saving himself was exactly how Jesus would save others. And in that perceptive moment he received one of the clearest promises of "salvation" in the Bible: "I tell you the truth, today you will be with me in paradise."

## REFLECTIONS

Whenever believers have doubted that Christ's death on the cross was enough to win God's forgiveness, cancel their judgment, and guarantee them a place in God's kingdom, Jesus' promise to a dying sinner has offered ample proof that he is the Saviour of all who humbly trust him.

This is what the young convict Samuel Peyton meant when he wrote to his mother almost eighteen hundred years later:

> Encouraged by the promises of that Saviour who died for us all, I trust to receive that mercy in the world to come, which my offences have deprived me of in this.

Peyton's hanging is mentioned in several journals at the time. It was a cold, wet, and squally June day. At 11:30 am the twenty-one-year-old mounted the gallows and made what one witness describes as "an eloquent and well directed speech" in which he admitted his guilt and asked forgiveness from those he had wronged. He "died penitent," says another witness. Christians would say he died in the embrace of the Saviour.

Christianity has always declared that Jesus died for petty thieves like Samuel Peyton, for Jewish rebels like the man crucified with Jesus, for neglectful materialists, for thankless atheists, for the morally self-righteous, and even for the smugly religious. For any who sincerely turn back to God, so says the New Testament and the Christian church ever since, Christ is the "Saviour who died for us all."

## A SELECTION OF READINGS ABOUT THE MEANING OF JESUS' DEATH

The New Testament offers many striking statements about the death of the Saviour. Here are just a few.

### Romans 3:21–26

But now apart from the law the righteousness of God has been made known, to which the Law and the Prophets testify. This righteousness is given through faith in Jesus Christ to all who believe. There is no difference between Jew and Gentile, for all have sinned and fall short of the glory of God, and all are justified freely by his grace through the redemption that came by Christ Jesus. God presented Christ as a sacrifice of atonement, through the shedding of his blood—to be received by faith. He did this to demonstrate his righteousness, because in his forbearance he had left the sins committed beforehand unpunished—he did it to demonstrate his righteousness at the present time, so as to be just and the one who justifies those who have faith in Jesus.

### Romans 5:6–10

You see, at just the right time, when we were still powerless, Christ died for the ungodly. Very rarely will anyone die for a righteous person, though for a good person someone might possibly dare to die. But God demonstrates his own love for us in this: While we were still sinners, Christ died for us. Since we have now been justified by his blood, how much more shall we be saved from God's wrath through him! For if, while we were God's enemies, we were reconciled to him through the death of his

Son, how much more, having been reconciled, shall we be saved through his life!

## 2 Corinthians 5:14–21

For Christ's love compels us, because we are convinced that one died for all, and therefore all died. And he died for all, that those who live should no longer live for themselves but for him who died for them and was raised again. So from now on we regard no one from a worldly point of view. Though we once regarded Christ in this way, we do so no longer. Therefore, if anyone is in Christ, the new creation has come: The old has gone, the new is here! All this is from God, who reconciled us to himself through Christ and gave us the ministry of reconciliation: that God was reconciling the world to himself in Christ, not counting people's sins against them. And he has committed to us the message of reconciliation. We are therefore Christ's ambassadors, as though God were making his appeal through us. We implore you on Christ's behalf: Be reconciled to God. God made him who had no sin to be sin for us, so that in him we might become the righteousness of God.

## Hebrews 9:11–28

But when Christ came as high priest of the good things that are now already here, he went through the greater and more perfect tabernacle that is not made with human hands, that is to say, is not a part of this creation. He did not enter by means of the blood of goats and calves; but he entered the Most Holy Place once for all by his own blood, thus obtaining eternal redemption. The blood of goats and bulls and the ashes of a heifer sprinkled on those who are ceremonially unclean sanctify them so that they are outwardly clean. How much more, then, will the blood of Christ, who through the eternal Spirit offered himself unblemished to God, cleanse our consciences from acts that lead to death, so that we may serve the living God! For this reason Christ is the mediator of a new covenant, that those who are called may receive the promised eternal inheritance—now that he has died as a ransom to set them free from the sins committed under the first covenant. In the case of a will, it is necessary to prove the death of the one who made it, because a will is in force only when somebody has died; it never takes effect while the one who made it is living. This is why even the first covenant was not put into effect without blood. When Moses had proclaimed every command of the law to all the people, he took the blood of calves, together with water, scarlet wool and branches of hyssop, and sprinkled the scroll and all the people. He said, "This is the blood of the covenant, which God has commanded you to keep." In the same way, he sprinkled with the blood both the tabernacle and everything used in its ceremonies. In fact, the law requires that nearly everything be cleansed with blood, and without the shedding of blood there is no forgiveness. It was necessary, then, for the copies of the heavenly things to be purified with these sacrifices, but the heavenly things themselves with better sacrifices than these. For Christ did not enter a sanctuary made with human hands that was only a copy of the true one; he entered heaven itself, now to appear for us in God's presence. Nor did he enter heaven to offer himself again and again, the way the high priest enters the Most Holy Place every year with blood that is not his own. Otherwise Christ would have had to suffer many times since the creation of the world. But he has appeared once for all at the culmination of the ages to do away with sin by the sacrifice of himself. Just as people are destined to die once, and after that to face judgment, so Christ was sacrificed once to take away the sins of many; and he will appear a second time, not to bear sin, but to bring salvation to those who are waiting for him.

## 1 Peter 2:20–25

If you suffer for doing good and you endure it, this is commendable before God. To this you were called, because Christ suffered for you, leaving you an example, that you should follow in his steps. "He committed no sin, and no deceit was found in his mouth." When they hurled their insults at him, he did not retaliate; when he suffered, he made no threats. Instead, he entrusted himself to him who judges justly. "He himself bore our sins" in his body on the cross, so that we might die to sins and live for righteousness; "by his wounds you have been healed." For "you were like sheep going astray," but now you have returned to the Shepherd and Overseer of your souls.

# 11

## ADAM:
## THE PROMISE OF HIS RESURRECTION

Concerning the resurrection of Jesus on Easter Sunday, I was for decades a Sadducee [a Jewish sect which denies the afterlife]. I am no longer a Sadducee since the following deliberation has caused me to think this through anew. . . . [W]hen these peasants, shepherds, and fishermen, who betrayed and denied their master and then failed him miserably, suddenly could be changed overnight into a confident mission society, convinced of salvation and able to work with much more success after Easter than before Easter, then no vision or hallucination is sufficient to explain such a revolutionary transformation. . . . If the defeated and depressed group of disciples overnight could change into a victorious movement of faith, based only on autosuggestion or self-deception—without a fundamental faith experience—then this would be a much greater miracle than the resurrection itself. In a purely logical analysis, the resurrection of Jesus is "the lesser of two evils" for all those who seek a rational explanation of the worldwide consequences of that Easter faith. (Pinchas Lapide, *The Resurrection of Jesus: A Jewish Perspective.* Eugene, OR: Wipf and Stock, 1982, 125–26.)

This quotation comes not from a clergyman or Christian scholar but from the late Professor Pinchas Lapide, a German historian of religion and Orthodox Jew. That a devout Jew, contrary to his own religious tradition, could conclude on historical grounds that Jesus rose again from the dead does not, of course, prove much. It does, however, illustrate something that may surprise some readers. The resurrection of Jesus remains a topic of serious enquiry among specialists in the field.

---

Specialists of all persuasions would agree that two of the most comprehensive tomes on the topic of the resurrection are (1) the massive volume by British New Testament historian N. T. Wright of the University of St. Andrews, *The Resurrection of the Son of God*. London: SPCK, 2003, and (2) the more recent one by Michael Licona, *The Resurrection of Jesus: A New Historiographical Approach*. Downers Grove, IL: InterVarsity Press, 2010. Both are works of impressive historical scholarship; both conclude the evidence favours an actual resurrection. For a far more skeptical conclusion, see Geza Vermes, *The Resurrection*. London: Penguin Books, 2008, or Gerd Ludemann, *The Resurrection of Christ: A Historical Inquiry*. Amherst, NY: Prometheus, 2004.

**BOOK NOTES**

---

It is not my intention to prove that Jesus rose from the dead: I have said all along, this is not that kind of book. I do, however, want to demonstrate that the resurrection is both an unavoidable theme of the earliest sources and an indispensable aspect of the Christian worldview ever since. It is no exaggeration to say that without the resurrection there is no Christianity. As the apostle Paul remarked in a moment of surprising candour: "if Christ has not been raised, our preaching is useless and so is your faith . . . we are of all people most to be pitied" (1 Corinthians 15:14, 19).

## RAISED EXPECTATIONS?

Prior to April AD 30 no one in the ancient world—Jewish or pagan—would have expected a crucified teacher such as Jesus to rise again from the dead. It was simply not part of anyone's job description for greatness. This point is frequently overlooked in popular discussions of the topic but it gives historians pause. The N. T. Wright book mentioned above lays out the evidence in detail and explores its implications.

It is true that some pagans celebrated rituals of dying-and-rising gods (typically as a symbol of the cycles of fertility and harvest), but no one in these cultures ever thought this was an event that took place in recorded history or that human beings themselves could experience this dying and rising. One famous dying-and-rising god is the Egyptian deity Osiris, who is revived by his wife (who is also his sister) Isis. The two then make love and give birth to other divinities. At no point in these myths were ancient pagans implying that such a thing happens in recorded history. This was a reality of the divine world whose historical reflection, or counterpart, isn't bodily resurrection but the renewal of agricultural harvest and human fertility. Indeed, scholars have often pointed out that such an idea would have been preposterous in Graeco-Roman thought since, for various complicated philosophical reasons having to do with the inherent inadequacy of bodily existence, pagans excluded the possibility of a post-mortem existence that was physical.

Unlike their pagan neighbours, many Jews in the period did believe in a bodily life after death. But they did so in a manner that would have militated against the expectation that someone would rise from the dead in AD 30. Traditional Jewish teaching, both before and after Jesus, stated that at the end of history the faithful dead would rise to eternal life in a divinely restored creation. This was a central part of the Jewish hope for God's future kingdom (which, you may remember from chapter 3, Jesus fully endorsed). Belief in a general resurrection in the "kingdom come" is everywhere in Jewish writings of the time: in the Dead Sea Scrolls, Josephus, the Pseudepigrapha, the Apocrypha, and elsewhere. To this day the future resurrection of the dead is a part of the official daily prayers of Orthodox Jews. The *Shemoneh Esrei* is the Jewish equivalent of Christianity's Lord's Prayer (or Our Father). It is meant to be prayed every day. Its second benediction reads:

> You are eternally mighty, my Lord, the Resuscitator of the dead are You; abundantly able to save, Who sustains the living with kindness, resuscitates the dead with abundant mercy, supports the fallen, heals the sick, releases the confined, and maintains His faith to those asleep in the dust. Who is like You, O Master of mighty deeds, and who is comparable to You, O King Who causes death and restores life and makes salvation sprout! (*Shemoneh Esrei 2*)

Belief in a future resurrection was founded on an important passage in the Old Testament book of Daniel (to which the above Jewish prayer alludes when it speaks of those "asleep in the dust"):

But at that time your people—everyone whose name is found
written in the book—will be delivered. Multitudes who sleep
in the dust of the earth will awake: some to everlasting life,
others to shame and everlasting contempt. Those who are
wise will shine like the brightness of the heavens, and those
who lead many to righteousness, like the stars for ever and
ever. But you, Daniel, roll up and seal the words of the scroll
until the time of the end. (Daniel 12:1–4)

The important point to observe is that resurrection in Judaism,
ancient and modern, is something that will happen at the conclusion
of human history, not in the middle of it. It is an event at "the
time of the end," as Daniel put it. Any claim that an individual
had experienced bodily resurrection before the arrival of God's
kingdom was not only unexpected, it was deeply counterintuitive
within a Jewish perspective. N. T. Wright puts the point forcefully
in his influential book on the topic:

[N]obody imagined that any individuals had already been
raised, or would be raised in advance of the great last day.
There are no traditions about prophets being raised to new
bodily life. . . . There are no traditions about the Messiah being
raised to life: most Jews of this period hoped for resurrection,
many Jews of this period hoped for a Messiah, but nobody
put these two hopes together until the early Christians did
so. It may be obvious, but it needs saying, however exalted
Abraham, Isaac and Jacob may have been in Jewish thought,
nobody imagined they had been raised from the dead. However important Moses, David, Elijah and the prophets may

have been, nobody claimed that they were alive again in the "resurrection" sense. The martyrs were honoured, venerated even; but nobody said they had been raised from the dead. The world of Judaism had generated, from its rich scriptural origins, a rich variety of beliefs about what happened, and would happen, to the dead. But it was quite unprepared for the new mutation that sprang up, like a totally unexpected claim, within the already well-stocked garden. (N. T. Wright, *The Resurrection of the Son of God*, 205–06)

The early Christian claim that their Saviour had experienced the future resurrection *in advance* (as it were) is a kind of "mutation," completely without precedent in both Jewish and Graeco Roman cultures of antiquity. Certainly, something other than existing expectations gave rise to the claim. So what was it?

Adding to the scholarly conundrum over what might have prompted the first Christians to make claims about a resurrection is what we know of Jewish martyrdom. Ever since the Jewish revolts against Greek domination in the 160s BC (called the Maccabean Wars), a strong tradition in Judaism paid special honour to faithful Jews slain by pagan overlords. Such people were praised in popular legends and their tombs became sites of religious veneration. By the time the Romans ruled Judaea (from 63 BC) this tradition was firmly established in Jewish consciousness. Scholars frequently comment upon the significance of this observation. If the New Testament had left Jesus in a martyr's tomb, this would have been a perfectly respectable way to conclude a story about a great Jewish teacher. There was no need, in other words, to invent a resurrection story in order to secure Jesus' fame. The fact that the pagan Romans executed him would have virtually guaranteed him a place in the roll call of faithful Jewish martyrs. Yet, from the earliest period, the disciples made no attempt to cast Jesus as a heroic martyr. And, so far as we can tell, his tomb was never a site of religious devotion. Instead, contrary to all expectations, the first Christians insisted that the tomb in which Jesus was laid on Friday afternoon was empty come Sunday morning.

Explanations abound, of course. Perhaps Jesus' followers stole the body and kept quiet about it all the way to their imprisonment and death (frequently by martyrdom). This was the Jewish leadership's counterclaim about the resurrection. Another popular explanation is that Jesus did not really die on the cross; he recovered from his injuries, walked out of the tomb, and convinced his disciples that God had granted him the glorious resurrection life awaiting all the faithful. Such explanations are rational only on the assumption, mentioned in chapter 3, that the observable laws of nature determine the parameters of what is possible in the universe. But, of course, the early Christians did not share this assumption. The empty tomb, combined with numerous reports that Jesus had appeared alive to his followers, convinced them that God had indeed raised his Messiah from the dead: the end-time resurrection had broken into history in the events surrounding Jesus. Their claim launched a movement that would utterly transform the world.

## THE EARLIEST RESURRECTION REPORT

As I mentioned earlier, reports about the resurrection appear throughout the range of our New Testament sources. At the end of the chapter I will offer some readings from the Gospels' resurrection accounts. For now, I want to focus on what historians regard as the most significant text about the resurrection.

In his letter to the newly founded church at Corinth, the apostle Paul reminds his converts of the core message (called the "gospel") he preached to them five years earlier. He does not expound the message in full; instead, he offers a fixed summary designed to recall the major elements of the preaching of the original apostles.

The verses quoted below contain what scholars universally regard as the earliest "creed" in Christianity. A creed is a pithy statement of what someone believes (*credo* is Latin for "I believe"). Some readers may have heard of the Apostles' Creed, which is said to this day in Roman Catholic and Protestant churches all over the world. The Apostles' Creed began to be formulated in the third century AD, but the creed found in Paul's letter to the Corinthians was composed and handed on to the apostle as early as AD 34, just a few years after Jesus' crucifixion. Paul (and others) used this creed as a bullet-point summary of their gospel. It was handed on to Christian communities as an official reminder of the founding message. Paul indeed describes it as something "of first importance":

> Now, brothers and sisters, I want to remind you of the gospel I preached to you, which you received and on which you have taken your stand. By this gospel you are saved, if you hold firmly to the word I preached to you. Otherwise, you have believed in vain. For what I received I passed on to you as of first importance:

that Christ died for our sins according to the Scriptures,
that he was buried,
that he was raised on the third day according to the
    Scriptures,
and that he appeared to Cephas, and then to the Twelve.

After that, he appeared to more than five hundred of the
brothers and sisters at the same time, most of whom are still
living, though some have fallen asleep. Then he appeared to
James, then to all the apostles, and last of all he appeared to
me also, as to one abnormally born. (1 Corinthians 15:1–8)

The above statement is significant for historians not simply
because part of it constitutes an eyewitness claim ("he appeared
also to me") but, more importantly, because of the date of the
report, early to mid-AD 30s in the opinion of most mainstream
scholars.

## HISTORY NOTE

How is this early creed dated? AD 33/34 is the date of Paul's first visit
to Jerusalem after his conversion (Acts 9:26–31) in AD 31/32 (Jesus'
death being dated in April AD 30). According to Galatians 1:18–19
Paul stayed with the apostle Peter during this fifteen-day visit and also
met with James the brother of Jesus. Paul must have received much
first-hand information about Jesus during this time (filling out what
he claimed had been revealed to him personally by the risen Jesus;
Gal 1:16). The creed Paul says he "received" (1 Corinthians 15:3) is

most likely to have been passed on to him during this visit, though some scholars prefer the earlier date (AD 31/32 in Damascus). For those interested in how scholars know any of these dates, including the date of Jesus' death, the scholarly benchmark is the book by Rainer Riesner, *Paul's Early Period: Chronology, Mission Strategy, Theology.* Grand Rapids: Eerdmans, 1998.

This early creed establishes beyond doubt that the claim about the resurrection belonged to the earliest stage of Christianity. It is not an extraneous belief inserted into the Gospels later; it was the bedrock of the Jesus-movement post AD 30. Whatever our personal feelings about "resurrections," there is no avoiding the historical conclusion that this claim has always been at the core of what we call Christianity. James Dunn of the University of Durham makes the point well:

> That belief seems to have been not only fundamental for Christianity as far back as we can trace, but also presuppositional and foundational. Any claims to disentangle a Jesus movement or form of Christianity which did not celebrate Jesus' resurrection inevitably have to assume what they are trying to prove, since all the data available (including Q) were retained by churches which did celebrate his resurrection. As a historical statement we can say quite firmly: no Christianity without the resurrection of Jesus. (Dunn, *Jesus Remembered*, 826.)

## RESURRECTION APPEARANCES AND AN EMPTY TOMB

According to 1 Corinthians 15:1–8 quoted above, the resurrected Jesus appeared to at least six different individuals or groups of disciples:

1. To Cephas, the Aramaic equivalent of the Greek name Peter;
2. To the Twelve apostles together;
3. To five hundred of the brothers and sisters at once;
4. To James, Jesus' brother;
5. To all of the apostles, that is, to missionaries beyond the group of the Twelve;
6. To the apostle Paul, who had been a persecutor of the Christians up to that moment.

Interestingly, there was another set of witnesses not mentioned in the above report. According to all four Gospels, the first people to witness the empty tomb and the risen Jesus were not the (male) apostles but a small group of women, including Mary (Jesus' mother), Salome, Joanna, and (another) Mary (Matthew 28:1–10; Mark 16:1–8; Luke 24:10–11; John 20:14–18). For historians, this is an intriguing detail, since the testimony of women was seriously questioned in both Jewish and Graeco-Roman cultures of the time. Josephus, writing in the first century, reflects the views of many in his day: "From women let no evidence be accepted, because of the levity and temerity of their sex" (*Jewish Antiquities* 4.219). Commenting on this detail James Dunn remarks:

> Yet, as is well known, in Middle Eastern society of the time women were not regarded as reliable witnesses: a woman's

testimony in court was heavily discounted. And any report that Mary had formerly been demon-possessed (Luke 8.2) would hardly add credibility to any story attributed to her in particular. Why then attribute such testimony to women— unless that was what was remembered as being the case? In contrast, can it be seriously argued that such a story would be contrived in the cities and/or village communities of first-century Palestine, a story which would have to stand up before public incredulity and prejudice? (Dunn, *Jesus Remembered*, 833.)

Put simply, if one were making up a story about a resurrection and wanting fellow first-century Jews to believe it, one would not include women as the initial witnesses. The point is worth reflecting on. It was once argued in scholarship that the Gospel accounts of the discovery of the empty tomb were late inventions crafted to lend narrative weight to the apostles' claims that they had seen Jesus alive. The view has lost favour over recent decades because several features of the accounts (the involvement of the women being just one example) suggest these narratives contain very early historical traditions. (By the way, "tradition," in the historian's sense of the word, does not mean a ritual or custom but a piece of officially preserved testimony about events). "The tradition history of the tomb and appearance narratives does not support the judgment that these are legends," writes Jens Schröter of Berlin's Humboldt University and one of the leading specialists of recent years. Rather, he says, "we are most likely dealing—as we also are with the report about the burial and resurrection witnesses—with an old tradition" (*Jesus of Nazareth*. Waco, TX: Baylor University Press, 2014, 207).

Whatever our personal feelings about the resurrection, it is difficult to avoid the historical conclusion that the empty tomb and the testimony of the women (along with that of the male apostles) were core parts of Christianity from its inception.

## WHAT HISTORIANS CAN AND CANNOT CONCLUDE

Let me repeat something I said in connection with Jesus' healings in chapter 3. By its nature, historical enquiry cannot determine whether a particular miraculous event took place. The best we can do is determine: (a) how early the reports about a supposed event are, i.e., whether the time gap between the event and the first report was sufficient for it to be explained as a mere "legend"; (b) how widespread the reports are, i.e., how many independent sources make the same claim; and (c) whether such claims can be explained by cultural expectation or precedent. In the case of the healings, you may remember, I stated that historians cannot affirm (or deny) Jesus actually healed anyone—that would be to go beyond historical method to philosophical interpretation. What historians can (and do) affirm is that the reports of Jesus healing people are early, widespread, and without clear precedent. This invites the mainstream conclusion that those around Christ interpreted his activities as supernatural.

Roughly the same historical conclusion can be reached about the resurrection. Historians cannot demonstrate that Jesus *actually* rose from the dead. (Whether we live in a universe created by a Being that can raise the dead is a philosophical question beyond the realm of historical investigation.) All they can do is demonstrate that the reports about the resurrection are early, widespread, and unique. Two conclusions are thus common among contemporary experts (regardless of their religious convictions):

1. Jesus' tomb was very likely empty shortly after his crucifixion, and;
2. From the very beginning, significant numbers of men and women claimed to have seen Christ alive from the dead.

How people account for these two historical data will depend largely on what one feels is possible in the world. As discussed in chapter 3, if I assume that the observable laws of nature define the limits of what is possible in the universe, then I can rationally affirm that no evidence will ever be good enough to overturn the conclusion that dead people stay dead. I will opt for whatever I believe to be the most plausible naturalistic interpretation. If, on the other hand, I assume that the laws of nature do not define the limits of what is possible in the universe—because there is a Lawgiver behind and above the laws of nature—then I can rationally interpret this historical data as evidence for an *actual* resurrection, at least in the case of Jesus (since no comparable data exist for any other character in history).

## HISTORY NOTE

A third conclusion can also be drawn from the data. Several of the key witnesses endured ill treatment and martyrdom rather than give up their claims about Jesus. The deaths of the apostles James, Peter, and Paul and that of James the brother of Jesus were discussed in chapter 5. The historical sources for these martyrdoms are Acts 12:1–2; Josephus, *Jewish Antiquities* 20.200; 1 Clement 5:1–7; and Eusebius, *Ecclesiastical History* 2.25.5–6. It is true that fanatics regularly give their lives for a cause they believe in. The difference with the first disciples, of course, is that they were in a position to know whether their "cause" was in fact based on a fabrication. Reflection on this point has led even the most skeptical to concede that the apostles really did believe they saw Jesus alive. The body-snatching "explanation" of the resurrection thus has very few adherents among specialists.

Whether one concludes that Jesus rose again depends in the end not on historical questions but (principally) on one's beliefs about God. Eminent New Testament scholar Professor Graham Stanton of Cambridge University puts the point bluntly. After traversing much of the same ground covered above, he concludes:

> The early Christian claim was that God raised the crucified, dead, and buried Jesus "on the third day" to a new form of existence, the precise nature of which Paul and the four evangelists describe in rather different ways. That claim can be neither confirmed nor denied with the use of historical lines of inquiry. Whether it may be accepted as plausible depends both on careful assessment of the resurrection traditions and on convictions about God. (Stanton, *The Gospels and Jesus*, 291)

## "ADAM": THE MEANING OF THE RESURRECTION

Readers may be wondering why I titled this chapter "Adam"—so far, I have said nothing about the ancient story of Adam and Eve told in the opening chapters of the Bible. The answer is perhaps surprising.

The first Christians interpreted the resurrection in a variety of ways as they began to make sense of something completely without precedent and entirely unexpected. Sometimes they said the resurrection was God's vindication of a prophet wrongly treated (Acts 3:13–15). Often they held it up as proof that Jesus was the Son of God, the Messiah (Romans 1:2–4). But one of the earliest and most significant interpretations is found in Paul's letter to the Corinthians, in a passage following on from the gospel creed discussed earlier. Here, the apostle says the resurrection establishes Jesus as the founding member of a revived humanity in God's long-awaited kingdom. Jesus, in other words, is the new "Adam":

> But Christ has indeed been raised from the dead, the firstfruits of those who have fallen asleep. For since death came through a man, the resurrection of the dead comes also through a man. For as in Adam all die, so in Christ all will be made alive. But each in turn: Christ, the firstfruits; then, when he comes, those who belong to him. Then the end will come, when he hands over the kingdom to God the Father after he has destroyed all dominion, authority and power. (1 Corinthians 15:20–24.)

There is so much we could explore in this passage (entire PhDs have been written on this section of Paul's letter). For my purpose only a few things are worth mentioning. First, Paul describes the risen Jesus as the "firstfruits," an agricultural term for the initial produce of a coming harvest. What does this mean? As a Jew, Paul had been brought up believing that resurrection was a future experience for the whole of humanity (the idea of departed souls entering an eternal, ethereal existence was pagan, not Jewish). Jews hoped for a resurrected humanity in a renewed creation. In the passage just quoted Paul is trying to reconcile this Jewish theology with his personal encounter with the risen Christ. Jesus, says Paul, is the *firstfruits* of God's great future harvest when he revives the dead and renews the world. What God had promised to do at the end of history, he has demonstrated within history in raising Jesus from the dead.

As the firstfruits Jesus is also a kind of "Adam" figure, Paul says. Again, the apostle is operating here in a thoroughly Jewish (Old Testament) frame of mind. According to the opening chapters of the Bible (Genesis 1:27–4:1), the entire history of humanity could be observed in the actions of the first human being. Adam was fashioned by the loving hands of the Creator only to turn his back on the Almighty, preferring personal autonomy to a relationship with God. The story of Adam eating from the "tree of the knowledge of good and evil" has nothing to do with gluttony or sensuality; it is all about man wanting to determine for himself, without God's involvement, what the parameters of "good and evil" should be. Whatever one's view of the origin of our species, the message of the Genesis narrative is profound and universal. This point is underlined by the fact that "Adam" in Hebrew means simply "man, mankind." Here is the truth about all humanity in a story about just one.

Paul's point in referring to this Old Testament narrative is clear. What Adam was to world history, Jesus is to God's future kingdom: the progenitor and paradigm of a new humanity. Jesus is the original of the species, as it were, and he determines our destiny.

Also important is Paul's mention of God's "kingdom." Here, Paul reflects both Jewish beliefs and Jesus' teaching. In chapter 3 we saw that Jesus proclaimed a future kingdom when all creation would be brought into conformity to the wise and loving purposes of the Creator. In this sense, he was perfectly in line with classical Judaism, ancient and modern. On one or two occasions, however, as we saw, Jesus said that the future kingdom was somehow present in his ministry of healing and exorcism: "the kingdom of God has come upon you," he said (Matthew 12:28). In other words, what was usually described in the Bible as an ultimate future reality could be glimpsed in Jesus' startling deeds. The apostle Paul says Christ's resurrection functions in a similar way. It is a glimpse of God's future kingdom. The Old Testament pledge to raise the dead and revive creation at the end of history finds a divine guarantee—a down payment, you might say—within history in the resurrection of the Messiah.

Far more than vindication of a righteous man or a proof of the Messiah, the resurrection of Jesus is the Creator's first act of bringing all creation into conformity with his purposes. It anticipates the day when, as Paul says above, Christ will have "destroyed all dominion, authority and power." Jesus is "Adam" in God's new kingdom.

## REFLECTIONS

From the very beginning, the resurrection of Christ shaped decisively the Christian view of the "afterlife." This is illustrated well by the Apostles' Creed, mentioned in passing earlier, which has been a standard statement of Christian belief since its origins in the third century. To this day Roman Catholics and Protestants affirm the Apostles' Creed, making it an extraordinarily ecumenical statement. In any case, there are two references in this creed to the "afterlife." One relates to Jesus in the past, the other to Christians in the future. Both concern the absolutely essential idea of *bodily* resurrection. To quote the creed in full (originally in Latin and Greek):

I believe in God, the Father Almighty,
maker of heaven and earth,
and in Jesus Christ,
his only Son, our Lord,
who was conceived by the Holy Spirit,
born of the virgin Mary,
suffered under Pontius Pilate,
was crucified, dead, and buried;
he descended to the dead.
*The third day he rose again from the dead;*
he ascended into heaven,
and is seated at the right hand of God,
the Father almighty.
From there he shall come to judge
the living and the dead.
I believe in the Holy Spirit,
the holy catholic church,
the communion of saints,
the forgiveness of sins,
*the resurrection of the body,*
and the life everlasting. Amen.

> ("Apostles' Creed." *An Australian Prayer Book.* Anglican Information Office, 1978, 200, modified.)

Sometimes even long-term churchgoers mistake the reference at the end of the Creed to the "resurrection of the body and the life everlasting" as a reiteration of what is said earlier about Jesus being raised. But the final lines of this ancient summary of Christian belief clearly refer to the believer, not Jesus. Following the teaching of the New Testament, the Creed states that just as "on the third day he [Jesus] rose again" so at the end of history men and women will experience "the resurrection of the body." And it is in that *bodily* mode that the faithful will enjoy "the life everlasting." Historically, the Christian view of the afterlife has always involved resurrected bodies in a revived creation. That is what the kingdom of God is.

Here we arrive at one of the distinctive elements of the biblical understanding of the future. Eastern traditions such as Hinduism and Buddhism respond to the frailties and disappointments of the natural order by holding out the eternal hope of *moksha* ("release") for the Hindu and *nirvana* (literally, "blown-out") for the Buddhist. Both involve a state of absolute non-physicality: "liberated," says the *Bhagavad Gita*, perhaps the most popular of all Hindu texts, "freed from all material contamination" (*Bhagavad Gita.* Translated by R. Gotshalk. Delhi: Banarsidass, 1985, 6.28).

---

Classical Hindu descriptions of the eternal, bodiless soul (*atman*) after death may be found in the *Katha Upanishad* 2.14–3.17 (see *Hindu Scriptures.* Translated by D Goodall. Berkeley: University of California Press, 1996, 173–76). While Buddhism rejects the notion of an eternal *atman*, its idea of *nirvana* is fundamentally bodiless. For an excellent exposition of this theme from the Buddha's own lips see *Aggi-Vacchagotta Sutta* ("Discourse to Vacchagotta on Fire"), Majjhima-Nikaya 72, from the *Sutta Pitaka* (*The Collection of the Middle Length Sayings*, vol. 2. Translated by I. B. Horner. London: The Pali Text Society, 1989, 162–67).

**BOOK NOTES**

For these Eastern philosophies, physical reality is no reality at all. The body is an entrapment from which we will finally free ourselves. Biblical hope is radically different. When the Bible describes the future kingdom of God—what we commonly call "heaven"—it speaks not of the removal of physical existence but of its re-creation. The natural world will be liberated and the human body redeemed. Consider these words from the apostle Paul:

> The creation itself will be liberated from its bondage to decay and brought into the freedom and glory of the children of God. We know that the whole creation has been groaning as in the pains of childbirth right up to the present time. Not only so, but we ourselves, who have the firstfruits of the Spirit, groan inwardly as we wait eagerly for our adoption to sonship, the redemption of our bodies. (Romans 8:21–23)

For many of us I suspect our picture of the "kingdom come" derives from an unlikely combination of ancient Greek philosophy and modern Hollywood movies. The ancient Greek philosopher Plato taught that the physical world is a kind of dim reflection of the ultimate non-physical reality toward which everything is destined. Somehow, Hollywood got hold of this idea and now almost always portrays the afterlife as a fourth-dimensional existence with clouds, halos, bright lights, and the ever-present harp music. "Bodies" are conspicuous by their absence.

In the years after I first learnt about Christ, it always troubled me that I was now meant to enjoy the thought of escaping the physical world and entering a spiritual one called heaven. I loved the taste, smell, sight, sound, and touch of this world, and now I was meant to look forward to losing those five senses and having them replaced by a spiritual sixth sense. I was not terribly excited about it.

Fortunately, I soon learnt that this was not what Christianity affirms about the afterlife at all. The biblical "kingdom come" is not an ethereal place of clouds and ghosts, but a tangible place of real existence. Far from the Hollywood notion of a disembodied, nirvana-like bliss, the Old and New Testaments promise a "new creation" and a "resurrection of the body" (see Isaiah 65:17–25 in the Old Testament and Revelation 20:11–21:5 in the New Testament).

The vision of the "kingdom come" that historic Christianity has proclaimed is not a ghostly existence, which denies the reality of creation, but a bodily existence in which the frailties and disappointments of the natural order are resolved through an extraordinary act of divine re-creation. If readers are wondering what all this has to do with the topic of Christ's resurrection, the answer is simple: Christ's rising to life is central to biblical faith not merely because it marks out his life as a unique moment in history but because in it God shows he is willing and able to breathe new life where there is currently death and disorder.

According to almost two millennia of Christian reflection on the bizarre events of April AD 30, the resurrection of Jesus is God's tangible pledge within history that he intends to do the same for the whole creation at the end of history. It is on this basis that Christianity from the earliest days proclaimed Jesus as the true "Adam" and invited the world to become part of the new humanity he has promised.

## A SELECTION OF READINGS ON THE RESURRECTION OF CHRIST

### Luke 24:1–47

On the first day of the week, very early in the morning, the women took the spices they had prepared and went to the tomb. They found the stone rolled away from the tomb, but when they entered, they did not find the body of the Lord Jesus. While they were wondering about this, suddenly two men in clothes that gleamed like lightning stood beside them. In their fright the women bowed down with their faces to the ground, but the men said to them, "Why do you look for the living among the dead? He is not here; he has risen! Remember how he told you, while he was still with you in Galilee: 'The Son of Man must be delivered over to the hands of sinners, be crucified and on the third day be raised again.'" Then they remembered his words. When they came back from the tomb, they told all these things to the Eleven and to all the others. It was Mary Magdalene, Joanna, Mary the mother of James, and the others with them who told this to the apostles. But they did not believe the women, because their words seemed to them like nonsense. Peter, however, got up and ran to the tomb. Bending over, he saw the strips of linen lying by themselves, and he went away, wondering to himself what had happened.

Now that same day two of them were going to a village called Emmaus, about seven miles from Jerusalem. They were talking with each other about everything that had happened. As they talked and discussed these things with each other, Jesus himself came up and walked along with them; but they were kept from recognizing him. He asked them, "What are you discussing together as you walk along?" They stood still, their faces downcast. One of them, named Cleopas, asked him, "Are you the only one visiting Jerusalem who does not know the things that have happened there in these days?" "What things?" he asked. "About Jesus of Nazareth," they replied. "He was a prophet, powerful in word and deed before God and all the people. The chief priests and our rulers handed him over to be sentenced to death, and they crucified him; but we had hoped that he was the one who was going to redeem Israel. And what is more, it is the third day since all this took place. In addition, some of our women amazed us. They went to the tomb early this morning but didn't find his body. They came and told us that they had seen a vision of angels, who said he was alive. Then some of our companions went to the tomb and found it just as the women had said, but they did not see Jesus."

He said to them, "How foolish you are, and how slow to believe all that the prophets have spoken! Did not the Messiah have to suffer these things and then enter his glory?" And beginning with Moses and all the Prophets, he explained to them what was said in all the Scriptures concerning himself. As they approached the village to which they were going, Jesus continued on as if he were going farther. But they urged him strongly, "Stay with us, for it is nearly evening; the day is almost over." So he went in to stay with them.

When he was at the table with them, he took bread, gave thanks, broke it and began to give it to them. Then their eyes were opened and they recognized him, and he disappeared from their sight. They asked each other, "Were not our hearts burning within us while he talked with us on the road and opened the Scriptures to us?"

They got up and returned at once to Jerusalem. There they found the Eleven and those with them, assembled together and saying, "It is true! The Lord has risen and has appeared to Simon." Then the two told what had happened on the way, and how Jesus was recognized by them when he broke the bread. While they were still talking about this, Jesus himself stood among them and said to them, "Peace be with you." They were startled and frightened, thinking they saw a ghost. He said to them, "Why are you troubled, and why do doubts rise in your minds? Look at my hands and my feet. It is I myself! Touch me and see; a ghost does not have flesh and bones, as you see I have." When he had said this, he showed them his hands and feet. And while they still did not believe it because of joy and amazement, he asked them, "Do you have anything here to eat?" They gave him a piece of broiled fish, and he took it and ate it in their presence.

He said to them, "This is what I told you while I was still with you: Everything must be fulfilled that is written about me in the Law of Moses, the Prophets and the Psalms." Then he opened their minds so they could understand the Scriptures. He told them, "This is what is written: The Messiah will suffer and rise from the dead on the third day, and repentance for the forgiveness of sins will be preached in his name to all nations, beginning at Jerusalem."

## John 20:1–29

Early on the first day of the week, while it was still dark, Mary Magdalene went to the tomb and saw that the stone had been removed from the entrance. So she came running to Simon Peter and the other disciple, the one Jesus loved, and said, "They have taken the Lord out of the tomb, and we don't know where they have put him!" So Peter and the other disciple started for the tomb. Both were running, but the other disciple outran Peter and reached the tomb first. He bent over and looked in at the strips of linen lying there but did not go in. Then Simon Peter came along behind him and went straight into the tomb. He saw the strips of linen lying there, as well as the cloth that had been wrapped around Jesus' head. The cloth was still lying in its place, separate from the linen. Finally the other disciple, who had reached the tomb first, also went inside. He saw and believed. (They still did not understand from Scripture that Jesus had to rise from the dead.)

Then the disciples went back to where they were staying. Now Mary stood outside the tomb crying. As she wept, she bent over to look into the tomb and saw two angels in white, seated where Jesus' body had been, one at the head and the other at the foot. They asked her, "Woman, why are you crying?" "They have taken my Lord away," she said, "and I don't know where they have put him." At this, she turned around and saw Jesus standing there, but she did not realize that it was Jesus. He asked her, "Woman, why are you crying? Who is it you are looking for?" Thinking he was the gardener, she said, "Sir, if you have carried him away, tell me where you have put him, and I will get him." Jesus said to her, "Mary." She turned toward him and cried out in Aramaic, "Rabboni!" (which means Teacher). Jesus said, "Do not hold on to me, for I have not yet ascended to the Father. Go instead to my brothers and tell them, 'I am ascending to my Father and your Father, to my God and your God.'" Mary Magdalene went to the disciples with the news: "I have seen the Lord!" And she told them that he had said these things to her.

On the evening of that first day of the week, when the disciples were together, with the doors locked for fear of the Jewish leaders, Jesus came and stood among them and said, "Peace be with you!" After he said this, he showed them his hands and side. The disciples were overjoyed when they saw the Lord. Again Jesus said, "Peace be with you! As the Father has sent me, I am sending you." And with that he breathed on them and said, "Receive the Holy Spirit. If you forgive anyone's sins, their sins are forgiven; if you do not forgive them, they are not forgiven."

Now Thomas (also known as Didymus), one of the Twelve, was not with the disciples when Jesus came. So the other disciples told him, "We have seen the Lord!" But he said to them, "Unless I see the nail marks in his hands and put my finger where the nails were, and put my hand into his side, I will not believe." A week later his disciples were in the house again, and Thomas was with them. Though the doors were locked, Jesus came and stood among them and said, "Peace be with you!" Then he said to Thomas, "Put your finger here; see my hands. Reach out your hand and put it into my side. Stop doubting and believe." Thomas said to him, "My Lord and my God!" Then Jesus told him, "Because you have seen me, you have believed; blessed are those who have not seen and yet have believed."

# 12

## CAESAR:
## HIS SUBVERSION OF AN EMPIRE

### THE EMPEROR AND HIS GOSPEL

Some will have heard before of the child born in the Roman Empire over two thousand years ago who would change the course of history, at least for a while. As the child grew, his charisma and power would command the loyalty of countless thousands. By the time he was in his thirties he would be seen as the fulfilment of national hopes and founder of an endless kingdom. His achievements would be considered miraculous, signs of divine authority, particularly the way he established peace in a period marked by chaos.

So significant was this man's entry into history that official proclamations, known as "gospels," were published throughout the world in his honour. One such proclamation was inscribed on stone and uncovered in Priene on the southwest coast of Turkey. It describes how the governor of the region decreed that the year of this Saviour's birth was henceforth to be known as Year 1 of a whole new calendar system. The inscription declares:

God sent him as a saviour for us to make war to cease, to create peaceful order everywhere. And the birthday of this "god" was the beginning for the world of gospels that have come to men through him. So, Paulus Fabius Maximus, the proconsul of the province of Asia [modern Turkey] has devised a way of honouring him, namely, that the reckoning of time for the course of human life should begin with the year of his birth.

The "saviour" I am describing is not Jesus, but Gaius Octavius, otherwise known as Caesar Augustus (63 BC–14 AD), the first emperor of Rome.

---

**BOOK NOTES** | The most complete copy of the Augustus decree comes from the Priene inscription (which is referenced as OGIS 2, 458), but fragmentary copies of the documents and accompanying letters for the decree also exist. For these see F. W. Danker. *Benefactor: Epigraphic Study of a Graeco-Roman and New Testament Semantic Field*. St. Louis: Clayton Publishing House, 1982, 215–27.

---

If my description of Emperor Augustus sounds strangely like an account of Christ, this is not (mainly) because of the spin I gave the retelling. Speaking of a "gospel" for humankind, a "saviour" sent by God and "peace" for the world were Roman imperial traditions long before they were part of the Christian vocabulary. And herein lies a window into a subtle but significant portrait of Jesus contained in the New Testament: the remarkable claim of the early Christians was that Jesus was, in a sense, the true emperor and Lord of the world.

# THE KINGDOM OF CAESAR VERSUS THE KINGDOM OF GOD

The opening paragraphs of the Gospel of Luke narrate the well-known story of the birth of Christ. The text is far more than the sweet scene sentimentalised in Christmas cards. Throughout the text Luke borrows long established imperial terminology and, like other New Testament writers, deliberately applies it to Jesus, the Jewish Messiah descended from King David and destined to rule the world forever. The gospel of Christ is here set over and against the gospel of Caesar. Chapter 2 of Luke's Gospel begins this way:

> In those days Caesar Augustus issued a decree that a census should be taken of the entire Roman world. (This was the first census that took place while Quirinius was governor of Syria.) And everyone went to their own town to register. So Joseph also went up from the town of Nazareth in Galilee to Judaea, to Bethlehem the town of David, because he belonged to the house and line of David. He went there to register with Mary, who was pledged to be married to him and was expecting a child. (Luke 2:1–5)

There were many censuses in the ancient world, but we do not have corroboration for this one. We know of a census a decade later (conducted by the same Quirinius). Luke seems to know of that one, too, and yet distinguishes it from the census he says occurred when Jesus was born: "This was the *first* census," he says, suggesting he knows of more than one.

The important thing to note, however, is that a census in Roman thought had little to do with assessing the distribution of health services or improving public transport. It was principally about Roman power and wealth. It was a way for the emperor to determine the number of his subjects and the amount of tax revenue he could expect.

Against this background, the mention of the Christ-child "belonging to the house and line of David" fires a subtle but unmistakable salvo across the bow of the imperial machinery. If this were the first time we had heard of the "line of David," we might have glanced over the reference as trivial—a simple genealogical detail. But Luke has already told us in chapter 1 what these references to David are all about. In the announcement to Jesus' mother Mary we read:

> You [Mary] will conceive and give birth to a son, and you are to call him Jesus. He will be great and will be called the Son of the Most High. The Lord God will give him the throne of his father David, and he will reign over Jacob's descendants [i.e., Israel] forever; his kingdom will never end. "How will this be," Mary asked the angel, "since I am a virgin?" . . . So the holy one to be born will be called the Son of God. (Luke 1:31–35)

This announcement recalls the fundamental Jewish hope of the era, that a descendant of King David would one day rule an *eternal* kingdom (discussed in chapter 5). There can be no missing the point, then, as we arrive at Luke chapter 2. Just as Emperor Augustus is flexing his imperial muscles around the world, Mary and Joseph are making their way to Bethlehem, the town of David, where Mary will give birth to the Messiah promised to David. The kingdom of Augustus is about to contend with the kingdom of David, the kingdom of God.

Especially striking is the claim that this descendant of David is to be hailed "Son of God." Many of us associate that title with Jesus alone. But people in the Roman Empire—Luke's first readers—all knew that the current bearer of that title was the emperor.

As the adopted son of the deified Julius Caesar, Emperor Augustus assumed the public title "son of the god Julius." The title was then passed to his heirs. Augustus's (adopted) son Tiberius was emperor from AD 14 to 37, for the entire period of Jesus' adulthood. He informed everyone in the empire—approximately fifty million of them—that he was "son of god" by inscribing it on the most used coin of the day. Every denarius (the labourer's daily wage) minted during his twenty-three-year reign—including the one I wear on a necklace around my neck bore the inscription: TI(BERIVS) CAESAR DIVI AVG(VSTI) F(ILIVS) AVGVSTVS: "Tiberius, Caesar Augustus, son of the god Augustus."

For ancient readers, then, Luke's presentation of Jesus as the Son of God entitled to an eternal throne sets up an immediate and potentially subversive contrast between the Roman emperor, with his pretensions to divine sonship, and the Davidic Messiah, God's true Son.

## THE EMPEROR, THE MANGER, AND THE CROSS

Lest we get carried away with this and think the Messiah has come to do battle with Rome, the circumstances of the birth of this Son of God make clear that his will be a very different kind of kingdom. Luke's Gospel continues the Christmas narrative in these words:

> While they were there, the time came for the baby to be born,
> and she gave birth to her firstborn, a son. She wrapped him
> in cloths and placed him in a manger, because there was no
> guest room available for them. (Luke 2:6–7)

Augustus was born into privilege. Jesus was born to peasants
and was laid in a "manger," an animal feeding area. Clearly, God
destined his Messiah for a very different kind of rule. It is the theme
Luke wishes to emphasize. The manger is a potent sign of the
kind of kingship Jesus would embody in his adulthood: he would
achieve his glory not through power and coercion but in humility.

Indeed, what is implied by the manger will be explicit at his
cross: this emperor wins allegiance through humble sacrifice. In this
context, it is worth reflecting on another passage, from the end of
Jesus' life, which also seems to challenge Roman pretensions about
the emperor. In the crucifixion narrative of Mark's Gospel we read:

> With a loud cry, Jesus breathed his last. The curtain of the
> temple was torn in two from top to bottom. And when the
> centurion, who stood there in front of Jesus, saw how he died,
> he said, "Surely this man was the Son of God!" (Mark 15:37–39)

It is beautifully ironic—and it is likely Mark intended his
readers to notice the irony—that at the moment of Jesus' death
on a Roman cross, a commander in the imperial army declares
the Jewish Messiah to be the "Son of God," one of the principal
titles of Emperor Tiberius. What Luke hints at in the beginning
of his Gospel, Mark makes plain in the climax of his Gospel:
from the manger to the cross, the true emperor rules in humility

and sacrifice. The values of Rome are turned upside down. To quote Paul Barnett, an Australian New Testament historian (and former bishop):

> That a Roman, for whom crucifixion was an unmentionable obscenity, declares a crucified Jew to be the Son of God is astonishing. Romans only applied that title to the Roman emperor, who was associated with power and triumph. But this soldier applies the title to Jesus—a poor, humiliated, crucified man. This represents an inconceivable reversal in values. (Paul Barnett, *The Servant King: Reading Mark Today*. Sydney: Aquila Press, 1991, 298.)

## THE GOSPEL OF EMPEROR CHRIST

The clash between the kingdom of Christ and the empire of Rome continues through Luke's Christmas narrative as he describes the first announcement, or "gospel," concerning the birth of Jesus. Sending out heralds to proclaim gospels concerning the emperor's achievements was common practice at the time of Jesus' birth. To recall the famous Priene inscription: "God sent him [Augustus] as a *saviour* for us to make war to cease, to create *peaceful* order every-where . . . [and] the beginning for the world of *gospels* ["good news"]."

Luke 2 describes a new "gospel" about a true "Saviour" who brings lasting "peace." All three terms appear in a single paragraph in the heavenly announcement to the shepherds:

> "Do not be afraid. I bring you *good news* [literally: "gospel"] that will cause great joy for all the people. Today in the town

of David a *Savior* has been born to you; he is the Messiah, the Lord. This will be a sign to you: You will find a baby wrapped in cloths and lying in a manger." Suddenly a great company of the heavenly host appeared with the angel, praising God and saying, "Glory to God in the highest heaven, and on earth *peace* to those on whom his favor rests." (Luke 2:10–14, italics added)

The point of all this is to say that the first Christians, and Luke among them, believed they were in possession of a new gospel about the true emperor of the world. His kingdom, they declared, would bring peace, not by crushing force but by his death and resurrection, through which he would restore us to God and bind us to one another in love. *The Routledge Encyclopedia of the Historical Jesus* contrasts the *Pax Romana* (the "peace of Rome") with the peace of Christ:

In Palestine, far from the centre of the Roman power, many Jews saw the Romans not as peacemakers but as oppressors. Heavy taxation, occasional Roman disregard for Jewish religious scruples, and a lively tradition of national resistance movements sparked the rise of the messianism and social banditry. . . . [T]he belief, well-attested in early Christianity, that the cross effects peace with God and erases enmity among humans certainly coheres with Jesus' message that, unlike the *Pax Romana*, true peace emerges not from violence but from the expression of divine love. (Timothy J. Geddert, "Peace." *The Routledge Encyclopedia of the Historical Jesus*. Edited by Craig A. Evans. London: Routledge, 2008, 450–51.)

At times this gospel sounded like a direct challenge to Caesar, and in a sense it was. When the apostle Paul was in Thessalonica (Northern Greece) in AD 49, nearly two decades after Jesus, his message caused a riot because of the seeming political implications. Paul's accusers in the city declared:

> "These men who have caused trouble all over the world have now come here. . . . They are all defying Caesar's decrees, saying that there is another king, one called Jesus." When they [the Roman officials] heard this, the crowd and the city officials were thrown into turmoil. (Acts 17:6–8)

The Christian gospel was (and is) subversive— not in a military sense but certainly in a social, intellectual, and moral sense. The gospel never said that someone else should be sitting on the throne in Rome, but it did insist that someone else held the throne of the human heart and mind. Caesar was due my taxes and civil respect, said the early Christian, but he was not entitled to my love and worship, and he had no claim over my ethics. Those privileges, declared this gospel, belong to Jesus alone, the true Son of the true God.

---

**BOOK NOTES**

Other New Testament writers develop the theme of Christ's lordship over Roman imperial claims (e.g., Philippians 1:27–2:11, 1 Peter 3:14–22, Revelation 13–19). Entire books have been written on the topic: for example, Richard A Horsley and Neil Asher Silberman, *The Message and the Kingdom: How Jesus and Paul Ignited a Revolution and Transformed the Ancient World.*

New York: Grosset/Putnam, 1997. Some claims about how subversive the first Christians were go too far, in my view, with just about everything they believed being interpreted as a challenge to imperial authority. Still, works like this helpfully underscore the interest of scholars in reading the New Testament evidence against the backdrop of the grand claims made by the Roman imperial machinery. More measured and accessible is the book by British scholar N. T. Wright, *What Saint Paul Really Said*. Oxford: Lion Books, 1997. In chapters 3 and 5 Wright offers an excellent account of the way the apostle Paul set Jesus over and against the Roman emperor.

Of course, once this message was detected on the imperial radar, Rome responded by trying to eradicate the followers of Jesus, crucifying them, burning them alive, and using them for sport in the colosseum and other public places. But the movement grew. In less than three centuries, and in a way that no one can really explain, Christianity began to capture the heart of Rome. In the year 100 there may only have been 7,000–10,000 Christians, by a standard scholarly estimate. By AD 200 that number had probably grown to 200,000. By AD 300 there were as many as five to six million Christians in the empire. And imagine the feeling among believers in the middle of the fourth century when Rome stopped producing coins inscribed "Caesar, son of God" and started minting coins marked with the first two Greek letters of "Christ," inscribed as X (the Greek letter *chi* or the "ch" in "Christ") and P (the Greek letter *rhō* or the "r" in "Christ"). Jesus was being praised in a manner once reserved for emperors. The outrageous idea put forward in the Gospels had become a reality. The kingdom, launched with a manger and a cross, had conquered an empire carved out with the sword.

---

The growth figures offered above are the more sober scholarly estimate offered in a remarkable new book about the "clash" between Christianity and Rome by Larry Hurtado, a well-known professor from the University of Edinburgh, *Destroyer of the Gods: Early Christian Distinctiveness in the Roman World*. Waco, TX: Baylor University Press, 2016. Other scholars have suggested that as many as half of the fifty to sixty million residents of the empire were Christians by the middle of the fourth century; e.g., Rodney Stark's *The Rise of Christianity*. New York: HarperCollins, 1997, 3–27.

**BOOK NOTES**

---

# REFLECTIONS

The New Testament portrait of Jesus as true emperor obviously has less sting in it for us than it would have for the people of the first few centuries. But the point of the portrait remains the same. The gospel of Christ, rightly understood, is still subversive. It calls on men and women to see Christ as eternal and primary and all human cultures as provisional and temporary. Seeing Christ as emperor involves doing the hardest thing of all: refusing to be a captive to one's culture.

As much as I like to think of myself as informed and clear visioned, I am very much a "citizen" of my particular time and place—my blip on the radar of history. The way I look at the world and live in it are shaped decisively by key social influences: the family I came from, the education I received, my income level, the friends I mix with, and the media I absorb. I am a product of a cultural outlook that is thoroughly Western, individualistic, materialistic, image obsessed, and comfort driven.

Today we might not have an imperial machinery trying to shape our lives, but we have a cultural machinery that more than makes up for that. This process of cultural "citizenization" is so subtle it is almost impossible to think objectively about our own perspective, to discern which bits of our world are true and good and which seem acceptable simply because we are accustomed to them. This is the slightly disturbing thing about studying history, by the way. You come across things from previous cultures that are shocking and horrible by our standards but that seem to have gone unnoticed or uncritiqued in their day. Think of Rome's treatment of women, its slavery, or its practice of "exposure" (discarding unwanted babies). The most disturbing thing about noticing these historical blights isn't that the Romans didn't notice them; it is the thought that perhaps there are aspects of my life and culture that are equally horrible but that we see as normal. Ponder this long enough and we are led to one of two conclusions about contemporary culture. Either we have evolved to a point of cultural purity, or there must be dark elements in our culture that, because of this process of "citizenization," we cannot see properly, but that later generations will describe as ignorance or evil the way we talk of Roman sins.

Seeing Jesus as emperor calls on us to rise above the culture of our day, to sit loosely to the claims of "empire," and give priority to the values of Christ's kingdom. In the New Testament this is called being citizens of heaven (Philippians 3:20). This expression recalls how important it was for ancient people to be "citizens" of the Roman empire. But it subverts the notion, asking believers to draw their sense of identity from God's kingdom, to pin their hopes on Christ's vision of the future, and to commit themselves to the *Pax Christi*, Christ's way of peace through the ethic of love.

Viewing Jesus as emperor means that no part of life is free from the claims of Christ. Whatever the practice of contemporary believers, historic Christianity has always insisted that Jesus doesn't just rule an ethereal dimension of our existence called "religion"— our prayers and church attendance. The imperial descriptions of Jesus remind us that he is Lord over *all* things, religious and secular, spiritual and physical, private and public. He has claims, so the New Testament insists, over my finances, my career, my politics, my sex life, my intellect, my leisure, my ambitions, and my family. In short, confessing Christ as emperor is about giving him free reign in one's life, knowing that all empires will pass into oblivion, while Christ's kingdom reigns eternal.

# 13

## GOD:
### HIS ONENESS WITH THE ALMIGHTY

## HOW JESUS BECAME GOD: A FAIRYTALE

It has been said that the doctrine of Christ's divinity, so important to the Christian church through the ages, was really just the result of a *vote*, and a relatively close vote at that.

As relations between Christians and pagans became increasingly tense, the fourth-century emperor Constantine needed a political masterstroke that would bind the empire together. He found it in a theological innovation designed to blend Christian devotion to the man Jesus with the pagan preference for worshipping divinities. The emperor proposed, so the story goes, that Jesus should be regarded as divine, a god in his own right.

The plan was brilliant. Not only would it blend Christian and pagan beliefs, it would provide Constantine with a powerful new political tool—a divine figure whose authority could not be challenged by the masses.

A great council of Roman Catholic bishops was convened in AD 325 in the city of Nicaea (now İznik in Turkey). The emperor put forward his idea, applied the appropriate political pressure and, with the smallest of margins, won the vote. From now on, declared the Council of Nicaea, Jesus is to be worshipped as "true God of true God, begotten, not made, of one being with the Father," as the church's Nicene Creed (still said today) declares. The Vatican was complicit in this new vision of Jesus because it gave them more power. Now they could claim to be the custodians not just of a great moral teacher but of an all-powerful deity.

All that was left to complete Constantine's plan was a small rewriting of the history books. With the help of the Vatican again, the emperor banned and burned the original Gospels about Jesus—those which spoke of him as merely human—and commissioned four newly edited Gospels, ones more supportive of the idea that Jesus was divine. These are the Gospels now in the New Testament.

I should stop this version of the Jesus-becomes-God story before fellow believers report me to church officials or my fellow historians alert my academic superiors. Almost nothing in this chapter so far could be described as factual. Indeed, readers may have recognised this account of Jesus' rise to divinity as that offered by the fictional academics, Leigh Teabing and Robert Langdon, in Dan Brown's bestselling 2003 novel *The Da Vinci Code*.

When I finally joined the eighty million people who bought this page-turner (that's more than the sales for *Harry Potter and the Half-Blood Prince*), I fully expected to find half-truth mixed with historical detail in a cleverly constructed, if somewhat controversial, account of Christian origins. In fact, I found a fairytale.

I cannot comment on the book's treatment of sixteenth-century art—though I understand art critics are as amused by the novel as historians. However, I can say that virtually everything said in the book about the first few centuries of Christianity is fictional. At one level, I should not have expected anything different. It is a novel, after all. And yet, the opening page of the book sends a rather mixed message: "All descriptions of artwork, architecture, documents and secret rituals in this novel are accurate." I can only imagine this statement was intended by the author as a literary device, a way of drawing readers into Brown's world of intrigue. For, frankly, in the case of the book's account of how Jesus came to be regarded as divine, I found only one detail that could be described as accurate—a date. The Council of Nicaea did in fact meet in the year 325.

Pretty much everything Brown's characters say about this ancient council and the New Testament is either baseless or the opposite of what historians generally conclude. To begin with, the Vatican had very little presence at the great Council of Nicaea. The bishop of Rome (the Pope) did not even attend—he sent two priests in his place. Of the 250 bishops participating in the discussions, only six were even Roman Catholics. The rest were Eastern Orthodox, from Egypt, Palestine, Syria, Turkey, and Greece. To describe the Nicaean Council as a Vatican conspiracy to gain power is wide off the mark.

Importantly, the discussion at Nicaea was not *whether* Jesus was divine, but in what manner. The council gathered, in part, to assess the views of a recent theologian named Arius. Arius had proposed a way of thinking about Jesus' divinity that fitted better with the pagan belief that what is infinite could never be contained in what is finite. The fullness of God in a man was unthinkable in Graeco-Roman philosophy. Arius insisted that the divinity of Jesus was derived from and subordinate to the infinite divinity of God the Father. Jesus was a bridge between the finite and infinite. This was a much more palatable idea in pagan thought. It was precisely against Arius's concession to Greek philosophical thinking that a majority of bishops at the Nicene Council re-affirmed their belief in Jesus' full divinity, despite the philosophical problems that created in the minds of educated pagans. Nor was the vote "close," as Brown says. Only two of the 250 bishops in attendance sided with Arius and refused to sign the agreed statement.

Another Dan Brown faux pas concerns the role of the emperor in all this. Constantine convened the council and gave the opening address but he neither chaired the eight-week meeting nor determined its theological direction. All the emperor wanted was an agreement. To quote the *Oxford Dictionary of the Christian Church*, the academic authority on such matters, "Constantine's main interest was to secure unity rather than any predetermined theological verdict" ("Nicaea, First Council of." *Oxford Dictionary of the Christian Church*. Edited by L. Cross and E. A. Livingstone. Oxford: Oxford University Press, 1997, 1144.)

Actually, Constantine did not have a strong preference in the matter of how to talk about Jesus' divinity. He thought the debate between Arius and the rest was rather trivial and distracting. As an emperor obsessed with social unity, he felt "wounded" by dissension in the church he had recently come to love: "How deep a wound did my heart receive in the report that divisions existed among yourselves," Constantine wrote to a bishop named Alexander and to the priest Arius himself. "And yet," he goes on, "having made a careful enquiry into the origin and foundation of these differences, I find the cause to be of a truly insignificant character, and quite unworthy of such fierce contention." His call for unity is plain: "My design then was, first, to bring the diverse judgments formed by all nations respecting the Deity to a condition, as it were, of settled uniformity. . . . If I should succeed in establishing, according to my hopes, a common harmony of sentiment among all the servants of God, the general course of affairs would also experience a change." In other words, if Constantine could establish peace among the churches, harmony would break out in the world generally. Whatever the soundness of that reasoning, it is clear from the sources that Constantine had little interest in the details of the debate about Christ's divinity and was motivated from start to finish by a desire for imperial harmony. ("Constantine's letter to Alexander the Bishop, and Arius the Presbyter," in Eusebius's *Life of Constantine* 2.64–73. In vol. 1 of *The Nicene and Post-Nicene Fathers*. Edited by Philip Schaff. 1886–1889. Peabody, MA: Hendrickson, 2004, 515–18).

Finally, it is frankly impossible to mount an argument that Constantine commissioned the four Gospels now in the New Testament in an effort to promote a divine Jesus. Arius and his supporters were using exactly the same four Gospels as their opponents. And we have manuscript copies of these Gospels that predate Constantine by more than a century (e.g., Papyrus 75 is dated to AD 200 and is housed in Switzerland's Bibliotheca Bodmeriana). Even highly skeptical scholars today date the composition of the Gospels to the first century. Constantine did bankroll the production of fifty copies of the Christian Scriptures, professionally handcrafted at the famous scriptorium of Caesarea (Israel), but he had *no* role in determining which books of the Bible should be included.

---

**BOOK NOTES** | Martin Hengel of the University of Tübingen (Germany) wrote a very important book on how, when, and why the four Gospels came to be revered in all quarters of the early church: *The Four Gospels*

---

*and the One Gospel of Jesus Christ*. San Antonio, TX: Trinity University Press, 2000. For a reliable scholarly account of how the New Testament came together into one book, or "canon," see the still-standard work of Bruce Metzger, *The Canon of the New Testament: Its Origin, Development, and Significance*. Oxford: Clarendon, 1997. On the details of Constantine's involvement in the development of the canon and debates about the divinity of Christ, see David L. Dungan, *Constantine's Bible: Politics and the Making of the New Testament* (Philadelphia: Fortress, 2007).

## JESUS' DIVINITY IN THE SOURCES

Far from being a pagan invention of a fourth-century emperor, belief in Jesus' full divinity—his oneness with the Father—is found everywhere in Christian literature from the first to the fourth centuries.

Even non-Christian texts attest to the early Christian belief in Jesus' divinity. In the middle of the second century the Greek intellectual Celsus pours scorn on Jesus:

> He tried his hand at certain magical powers . . . and on account of them gave himself the title of God. (Origen, *Contra Celsum*. Translated by Henry Chadwick. Cambridge: Cambridge University Press, 1953, 1.28)

More significant is a letter from the Roman administrator Pliny to Emperor Trajan. The letter can be dated to AD 110—two centuries before Constantine. In the letter Pliny seeks advice on whether to keep executing the followers of Jesus. He tells the emperor that his interviews with Christians, which he says involved the torture of two leading women of the church, revealed only the following "crime":

> The sum total of their guilt or error was no more than the following. They had met regularly before dawn on a determined day, and sung antiphonally (i.e., alternately by two groups) a hymn to Christ as to a god. (Pliny, *Letters,* 10.96)

This text confirms what we know from our New Testament documents. In a departure from both Jewish and pagan thinking, the early Christians worshipped the man Jesus as the embodiment of divinity.

What is doubly fascinating is that we have at least two "hymns to Christ as God," as Pliny calls them, preserved in the earliest documents of the New Testament itself—the letters of Paul. Paul's letters were composed even before the Gospels so, in historical terms, they are highly significant sources for earliest Christianity. In his letter to the Christians at Colossae (southwestern Turkey) Paul offers a two-paragraph poem lauding Jesus in phrases such as:

> [Christ] is the image of the invisible God . . .
> For in him all things were created . . .
> For God was pleased to have all his fullness dwell in him
> [the Infinite in the Finite]. (Colossians 1:15, 16, 19)

There is debate about whether Paul composed this hymn himself or merely quoted what was already a well-known song of praise (or teaching poem). For our purposes that does not matter. All I want us to notice is that in our earliest Christian writings Jesus is already worshipped as the singular embodiment of God's invisible fullness.

## HISTORY NOTE

I should point out that the word "hymn" may be misleading. The first Christians probably didn't compose anything like the rhyming, melodious songs of modern "hymns" or "praise and worship." They were more influenced by the Jewish and biblical psalms, whose poetic flavour is less lyrical and whose musical form was probably closer to chanting than singing.

Another "hymn to Christ as God" is found in the apostle Paul's letter to the church at Philippi (northern Greece). The poetry of the Greek text cannot be seen in English translation, but most modern Bibles set the passage out in hymnic stanzas (like the following). Paul introduces it with "In your relationships with one another, have the same mindset as Christ Jesus," and then lets the hymn do the talking:

> Who, being in very nature God,
>> did not consider equality with God something
>>> to be used to his own advantage;
> rather, he made himself nothing

by taking the very nature of a servant,
being made in human likeness.
And being found in appearance as a man,
he humbled himself
by becoming obedient to death
—even death on a cross!
Therefore God exalted him to the highest place
and gave him the name that is above every name,
that at the name of Jesus every knee should bow,
in heaven and on earth and under the earth,
and every tongue acknowledge that Jesus Christ is Lord,
to the glory of God the Father.

(Philippians 2:5–11)

There is so much we could explore in these intriguing words—particularly the theme of Christ as servant, which we will study in the final chapter of the book. For now, I want us to notice how the hymn begins and ends: with the claim that Christ shares the nature and name of God. Prior to Christ's entry into the world he was "in very nature God." He enjoyed "equality with God," though he relinquished this status in his earthly ministry and suffering narrated in the next few sentences.

After Christ's service to humanity, declares this hymn, God "exalted him to the highest place and gave him the name that is above every name." The "name" referred to here is not the name "Jesus"; it is the name of God himself, Yahweh, translated in most English Bibles as LORD. The Old Testament background of the final stanza makes that clear. In the book of Isaiah God himself declares:

> By myself I have sworn, [says the LORD],
>> my mouth has uttered in all integrity
>> a word that will not be revoked:
>> "Before me every knee will bow;
>>> by me every tongue will swear."

(Isaiah 45:23)

The final lines of Paul's hymn take this Old Testament statement by God and apply it to the exalted Messiah:

> At the name of Jesus every knee should bow,
>> in heaven and on earth and under the earth,
>> and every tongue acknowledge that Jesus Christ is Lord.

The promise of God's universal lordship contained in the book of Isaiah is fulfilled, says this New Testament hymn, when every knee bows before and every tongue confesses Jesus as Lord. He is the one who shares the nature and name of the Almighty.

---

**BOOK NOTES**

Recently, well-known biblical scholar Bart Ehrman wrote a book questioning whether the New Testament teaches that Jesus is divine, arguing, instead, that Jesus is more an "angelic" figure than "God": *How Jesus Became God: The Exaltation of a Jewish Preacher from Galilee*. San Francisco: HarperOne, 2014. Ehrman is known for his independent views on various historical matters, and several scholars offered a detailed critique in a response volume edited by Michael F. Bird, *How God Became Jesus:*

*The Real Origins of Belief in Jesus' Divine Nature—A Response to Bart D. Ehrman*. Grand Rapids: Zondervan, 2014. Another important scholar who has worked on the same theme for decades is University of Edinburgh's Larry Hurtado. See his *How on Earth Did Jesus Become God? Historical Questions about Earliest Devotion to Jesus*. Grand Rapids: Eerdmans, 2005. This book is a popular-level distillation of his numerous contributions.

## JESUS' DIVINITY IN THE GOSPELS

What is sung in these New Testament hymns is also narrated in a variety of ways in the New Testament Gospels. At the simplest level, we could turn to statements in the Gospel of John. In one well-loved passage, Philip pleads with Jesus for a clear account of God the Father:

Philip said, "Lord, show us the Father and that will be enough for us." Jesus answered: "Don't you know me, Philip, even after I have been among you such a long time? Anyone who has seen me has seen the Father." (John 14:8–9)

The claim here is similar to that contained in the first New Testament hymn quoted above: Jesus is "the image of the invisible God."

We could also turn to the end of John's Gospel where the doubting Thomas sees the risen Jesus and makes a confession perfectly aligned with the second hymn quoted above. Titles normally reserved for the Almighty ("God" and "Lord") are applied to Jesus:

> Then he said to Thomas, "Put your finger here; see my hands. Reach out your hand and put it into my side. Stop doubting and believe." Thomas said to him, "My Lord and my God!" Then Jesus told him, "Because you have seen me, you have believed; blessed are those who have not seen and yet have believed." (John 20:27–29)

There are modern-day followers of the fourth-century Arius who try to avoid the implication of a passage like this. The Jehovah's Witnesses, for example, whom many readers will have met at their front door over the years, regard Jesus merely as an angelic being. They thus interpret Thomas's words here as an exclamation in the presence of Jesus rather than one directed toward him—a kind of "Oh my God!"—turning the proverbial doubting Thomas into blaspheming Thomas! Unfortunately, the original Greek of the relevant sentence is perfectly clear: *eipen autō* means "said *to him*" ("my Lord and my God").

It is because of statements like these, along with those in the New Testament hymns quoted earlier, that the Council of Nicaea rejected the more plausible pagan belief in a semi-divine Jesus and re-affirmed the Jesus who was "of one being with the Father."

The New Testament statements pointing to Jesus' oneness with God number about a dozen by my count (Matthew 1:23, 28:18–20; John 1:1, 1:14; 10:32–38; 14:9; 20:27–29; Romans 8:9–11; 1 Corinthians 8:5–6; 2 Corinthians 13:14; Philippians 2:6–11; Colossians 1:15–20; Revelation 22:12–13). But I want to conclude the argument of this chapter by outlining a more subtle, though perhaps more important, basis for the early Christian belief that Jesus was "in very nature God." It has to do with the topic of chapter 8 in this book, Jesus as *temple*.

Without going over the details again, readers will recall that Jesus set himself over and in place of the great Jerusalem temple—the locus of God's presence and mercy. In a huge claim to authority, he cleared the temple of its priestly merchants, and when asked for a sign of his authority to do such a thing he replied that he would destroy the temple and rebuild it in three days, at which point John's Gospel adds, "the temple he had spoken of was his body" (John 2:13–22). Again, in Matthew's Gospel, Christ compared his disciples to the temple priests and said of himself, "something greater than the temple is here" (Matthew 12:5–6). Equally revealing is that Christ boldly usurped the function of the temple whenever he handed out God's forgiveness on his own authority. The religious leaders knew exactly what this implied and protested: "Who is this fellow who speaks blasphemy? Who can forgive sins but God alone?" (Luke 5:20–21). In short, Jesus was a mobile temple, a one-man locus of the divine presence and mercy.

From the historical point of view, the early worship of Jesus as the embodiment of God may, in part, be traced to Jesus' own daring identification of himself with God's dwelling place, the temple. To quote N. T. Wright, a leading British historical Jesus scholar:

> My conclusion from this brief survey of the evidence is that Jesus believed himself called to act as the new Temple. When people were in his presence, it was as if they were in the Temple. But if the Temple was itself the greatest of Israel's

incarnational symbols, the conclusion was inevitable (though the cryptic nature of Jesus' actions meant that people only gradually realised what he had in mind): Jesus was claiming, at least implicitly, to be the place where and the means by which Israel's God was at last personally present to and with his people. Jesus was taking the huge risk of acting as if he were the Shekinah [divine glory] in person, the presence of YHWH [God himself] tabernacling with his people. (N. T. Wright, *The Challenge of Jesus*, 113–14)

The doctrine of Christ's full divinity was not a pagan outcome of fourth-century politics. It was implied by Jesus himself, sung about in the earliest Christian hymns, defended at the Council of Nicaea, and reaffirmed by all mainstream believers, Orthodox, Roman Catholic, and Protestant, ever since.

## REFLECTIONS

What are the implications of the New Testament affirmation that Jesus Christ embodied the Almighty? Let me offer an analogy, based on a true story, and then bring this chapter to a close.

Some of you may have heard before about a young woman raised in a small town outside Rio de Janeiro. Christina had always longed to experience the bright lights and party atmosphere of Brazil's famous city, but her mother had often warned her off— unemployment in the city was high; strip joints and brothels were just about the only places offering jobs to young women.

Christina did not listen. One day she packed her bags and secretly took off to the city. Terrified at what might become of her daughter, Christina's mother set out to find her. She searched the vast city in vain. Fearing the worst, she visited some of Rio's sleaziest establishments. And on the walls of these places she pinned photos of herself. On the back of each photo she wrote a simple message pleading with her daughter to come home: "Whatever you have done. It doesn't matter. Please come home."

Christina did eventually find herself employed in a Rio brothel. She was too ashamed to go home and, even if she wanted to, she was unsure her mother would take her back. One day, Christina was stumbling down the stairwell of one of these places when she noticed on the wall a photo of her mother. She took the image and read the message. And in that moment gazing down at her mother's image her confusion evaporated. The photo said it all. She returned home at once.

The doctrine of Christ's divinity declares that God has left a photo of himself in the world. From the first to the twenty-first century, Christians have claimed that in the life, teaching, miracles, death, and resurrection of Jesus, we see God. In the words of the New Testament hymn quoted earlier, "He is the image of the invisible God." Christ's life, in other words, clarifies the character and intentions of the Creator.

Throughout the centuries, this idea has brought comfort for some; for others, a challenge. For those with theological dilemmas and life experiences which have distorted their picture of God, looking to Christ—the photo of God—has brought the Almighty back into focus. They find in him a picture of the Creator in all his grace, gentleness, and love. In other words, what you see in Jesus is what you get with God. "Anyone who has seen me," says Jesus in John's Gospel, "has seen the Father."

For millions of people throughout the centuries this has been an enormous comfort.

But there has also always been a challenge in this New Testament theme. Many people through the ages have preferred to cherry-pick their image of God—a little bit of this, an adjustment of that, and so on. However, if, as mainstream Christianity affirms, God has revealed himself in the life of Christ, this tendency to pick and choose is relegated to the level of wishful thinking or even self-flattery. The doctrine of Christ's divinity insists that men and women are not at liberty to fashion a god of their own liking. God has made himself known on his own terms.

# 14

## SERVANT:
### HIS PREFERENCE FOR THE LOWLY

## THE CHRISTIAN BLASPHEMY

I once gave a talk at the University of Western Sydney on the theme of the last chapter, the divinity of Christ. I focused on the crucifixion narrative and underlined for the audience the striking nature of historic Christianity's claim that the Creator of the universe would condescend to take on flesh and suffer at the hands, and for the sake, of his creatures. After the talk the chairperson opened the floor for questions. A man in his mid-thirties stood up and proceeded to tell the audience how preposterous was the idea that the King of the universe could be subservient to the forces of his own creation. God is all-powerful and all-knowing, he declared: How could the Almighty experience frailty and suffering?

It turned out that the man was a Muslim leader at the university and an academic. His monologue was probably the longest five minutes of my speaking career. He was very civil but was adamant that what I had said was illogical: the Creator and Sustainer of all things could not possibly be dependent on earthly sustenance. In his mind, Jesus' need for earthly food was a knockdown argument against his divinity. More seriously, he insisted that what I had said was blasphemy because I had associated infinite majesty with human weakness and servitude. Only later did I realise these were traditional Islamic arguments against the Christian understanding of Jesus. They come straight out of the Qur'an itself:

> They do blaspheme who say, "God is Christ, the son of Mary." If they desist not from their word of blasphemy, verily a grievous penalty will befall the blasphemers. Christ the son of Mary was no more than an apostle. His mother was a woman of truth. They both had to eat their daily food. See how God makes his signs clear to them; yet see in what ways they are deluded. (Q Al-Maidah 5:72–75)

When the chairperson invited me to respond, I did my best to address his main concerns. But it soon became obvious there would be no "winner" in this debate. Our premises were miles apart. His vision of a majestic God excluded, by definition, any notion of weakness and servanthood. My vision of God's majesty consisted precisely in the Creator's willingness to serve his creation.

I ended simply by thanking my Muslim friend for drawing to the audience's attention a profound difference between Islam and Christianity. What is blasphemous to the Muslim is glorious for the Christian: God entered his creation to serve his creatures.

## DIVINE HUMILITY

There is perhaps no better biblical statement of this theme than the ancient Christian hymn preserved by Paul in his letter to the

Philippians, discussed in the previous chapter. I hope you don't mind if I quote it in full again:

> Who, being in very nature God,
>> did not consider equality with God something to be
>>> used to his own advantage;
> rather, he made himself nothing
>> by taking the very nature of a servant,
>> being made in human likeness.
> And being found in appearance as a man,
>> he humbled himself
>> by becoming obedient to death
>>> —even death on a cross!
> Therefore God exalted him to the highest place
>> and gave him the name that is above every name,
> that at the name of Jesus every knee should bow,
>> in heaven and on earth and under the earth,
> and every tongue acknowledge that Jesus Christ is Lord,
>> to the glory of God the Father.
>
> (Philippians 2:5–11)

In the history of Christianity, the theme of Christ's divinity has always been viewed from two angles. On the one hand, understanding Jesus to be "in very nature God" has inspired believers to marvel at his majesty. They confess that he is far more than a teacher, healer, saviour, and friend; he is the Lord over all and the one before whom every knee will bow.

Christ's divinity can be viewed from another angle. Pondering Jesus as the embodiment of God has led believers to marvel at the divine *humility*: in Christ, so the Christian church has affirmed, God is seen to be far more than Creator, Sustainer, and Judge; he is revealed to be the Servant, willing to put humanity's good before his own glory.

This is precisely where the accent of the above passage falls. Although it begins and ends on a note of glory, the heart of the text concerns Christ's *emptying* of himself to serve the needs of others. Lines 1 and 5 of the hymn highlight this mystery in an obvious way:

> *Who, being in very nature God,*
> > did not consider equality with God something to be
> > used to his own advantage;
> rather, he made himself nothing
> > *by taking the very nature of a servant.*

According to this early Christian confession, the one who is "in very nature *God*" took on the "very nature of a *servant*." The parallel is deliberate and striking. There are two words for "servant" in the original Greek. One refers to a "servant" with rights (*diakonos*), the other to one without rights (*doulos*). The second is usually translated "slave." And this is the term used above. The explanatory "made himself nothing" suggests that we need to give the term its full weight—God in Christ became a "slave."

The English Bible translators appear to have baulked at using the word "slave" to describe the One who is "in very nature God." But such squeamishness is inappropriate in Christianity. Unlike the Qur'an, the New Testament has no problem envisaging the Lord of all serving his creatures.

In any case, the language of "slavery" comes straight from Jesus' own description of his ministry. It is just possible this hymn found in Paul's letter to the Philippians recalls the words of Christ found in the Gospel of Mark:

> You know that those who are regarded as rulers of the Gentiles lord it over them, and their high officials exercise authority over them [in Roman-ruled Galilee and Judaea, this was a visible, daily reality]. Not so with you. Instead, whoever wants to become great among you must be your servant, and whoever wants to be first must be slave [*doulos*] of all. For even the Son of Man [Jesus himself] did not come to be served, but to serve, and to give his life as a ransom for many. (Mark 10:42–45)

It is difficult to convey just how radical this notion would have seemed to the first disciples. To be sure, in a few years Christians would be singing hymns about Christ the servant (such as Paul recounts), but before Jesus' death and resurrection the idea that greatness consists in humble service was not on the religious radar—not in the Egyptian mystery cults, nor Graeco-Roman religions, nor even in Judaism.

I was involved in a research project at Macquarie University exploring the origins of the virtue of humility. While nowadays we take for granted that humility is a desirable quality, in the ancient world this was not so. Humility before the gods and the socially powerful was valued, but lowering yourself before an equal (our working definition of humility) was considered undignified. After all, one of the chief goals of ancient Mediterranean life was to attain public honour for yourself and your family.

The first writings in antiquity to emphasise humility over honour were the New Testament texts. And the reason seems clear. The radical idea at the centre of these texts was that the Messiah and Lord was also the "slave of all." He came not to "be served, but to serve, and to give his life as a ransom for many." The cross, in other words, changed everything. If the highest Lord won his greatest achievement on a shameful cross, what else could it imply than that true glory consists in humble service! (My publisher will insist at this point that I mention a book I wrote on this topic a few years ago: *Humilitas: The Lost Key to Life, Love, and Leadership* [Grand Rapids: Zondervan, 2011]. I now regard it as my most misguided project. Who writes a book on humility?)

The night before his death on a cross, according to the Gospel of John, Jesus foreshadowed the servant theme in quite a shocking way. He did for his disciples what in antiquity only a household slave would do:

> Jesus knew that the Father had put all things under his power, and that he had come from God and was returning to God; so he got up from the meal, took off his outer clothing, and wrapped a towel around his waist. After that, he poured water into a basin and began to wash his disciples' feet, drying them with the towel that was wrapped around him. He came to Simon Peter, who said to him, "Lord, are you going to wash my feet?" Jesus replied, "You do not realize now what I am doing, but later you will understand." "No," said Peter, "you shall never wash my feet." Jesus answered, "Unless I wash you, you have no part with me." . . . When he had finished washing their feet, he put on his clothes and returned to his

place. "Do you understand what I have done for you?" he asked them. "You call me 'Teacher' and 'Lord,' and rightly so, for that is what I am. Now that I, your Lord and Teacher, have washed your feet, you also should wash one another's feet. I have set you an example that you should do as I have done for you." (John 13:3–8, 12–15)

I have often heard preachers challenge their audiences with lines like: imagine if God Almighty appeared before you right now in all his glory! The implication is that we would all feel humbled. True enough, I suppose. But more humbling by far, I think, would be the experience of the first disciples. Imagine observing the One you revered as the epitome of greatness taking off his robe, tying a towel around his waist, and doing for you what you had only ever seen a slave do for his master: without gimmick or guile he washes and dries your feet.

In the context of John's Gospel, Jesus washing the disciples' feet was intended, in part, as a picture of the humble service he would perform the following day as he suffered and died for humanity's salvation. But it was not merely a picture or theological illustration. The washing of the disciples' feet was intended as a potent example of the Christian life itself: "I have set you an example," Jesus said to his stunned disciples. Or, to quote Mark's Gospel again, "whoever wants to become great among you must be your servant." Christian life, as well as Christian theology, is based on and characterised by the servanthood that Jesus showed.

The hymn of Philippians quoted earlier makes exactly the same point. The apostle Paul did not include this passage simply so that his readers would sing about the "Lord" who became a "slave"; he included it because he wanted them to embody that mystery in their daily lives. The apostle introduces the hymn in the words:

> Do nothing out of selfish ambition or vain conceit. Rather, in humility value others above yourselves, not looking to your own interests but each of you to the interests of the others. In your relationships with one another, have the same mindset as Christ Jesus: [and so the hymn begins] Who, being in very nature God . . . made himself nothing, taking the very nature of a servant. (Philippians 2:3–7)

*Christology*— the study of the person of Christ—is intimately connected to Christian living. Knowing Christ will result in living Christianly; we should, Paul says, "have the same mindset as Christ Jesus," the servant. It is as simple and as difficult as that!

## REFLECTIONS

At various points throughout this book I have mentioned the incredible expansion of Christianity in its first three centuries. What started as a small group of Jews soon became the largest single social movement in the empire (perhaps in world history), winning people by the irresistible force of compassion and persuasion. To recall the conclusion of Rodney Stark, Professor of Sociology at Baylor University:

> The notion that the gods care how we treat one another would have been dismissed as patently absurd. . . . This was the moral climate in which Christianity taught that mercy is one of the

primary virtues—that a merciful God requires humans to
be merciful. . . . This was revolutionary stuff. Indeed, it was
the cultural basis for the revitalization of the Roman world.
(Stark, *The Rise of Christianity*, 209–15.)

The crowning symbol of Christian expansion—of the "revital-
isation of the Roman world," as Stark puts it—was the conversion
of the emperor himself. Constantine the Great (AD 272–337)
embraced Christianity sometime around AD 312. He applied his
new-found faith to matters of state bringing far reaching benefits
to ordinary citizens. He did not impose Christianity on the empire.
His approach was simply to end the persecution of Christianity and
grant the church the rights of any other religion or civic association.
But he did "Christianise" (if there is such a thing) certain Roman
laws. He humanised the criminal law and the law of debt, eased
the conditions of slaves, and, importantly, introduced imperial
financial support for children of poor families. The effect of this
last measure was to discourage the common Roman practice of
"exposure," abandoning unwanted babies. With the conversion of
Constantine, the empire established by brute force was beginning
to be conquered by the message of a Servant Lord.

## HISTORY NOTE

It is sometimes said today that Constantine made Christianity "the
state religion" and that he attempted to root out the Greek and Roman
religions and philosophies. In fact, he had a very cautious approach
to paganism. He did publish edicts declaring his love of Christ and

his hope that Romans would give up the error of polytheism, but he made clear—in the same edicts—that everyone should follow their conscience. In a proclamation to the provinces, he declared:

> My own desire is, for the common good of the world and the advantage of all mankind, that Thy people [Christians] should enjoy a life of peace and undisturbed concord. So let those who still delight in error [the pagan majority] be made welcome to the same degree of peace and tranquility which those who believe have. For it may be that this restoration of equal privileges to all [i.e., the removal of repressions of the Church] will prevail to lead them [pagans] into the straight path. Let no one molest another, but let every one do as his soul desires. . . . We pray, however, that they [pagans] too may receive the same blessing, and thus experience that heartfelt joy which unity of sentiment inspires. . . . Once more, let none use that to the detriment of another which he may himself have received on conviction of its truth; but let everyone, if it be possible, apply what he has understood and known to the benefit of his neighbour. ("Constantine's Edict to the People of the Provinces on the Error of Polytheism," *Life of Constantine* 2.56 in *The Nicene and Post-Nicene Fathers*, 512–14.)

For a very brief but authoritative account of Constantine's conversion and its implications for the church, see "Constantine the Great." *Oxford Dictionary of the Christian Church.* Edited by F. L. Cross and E. A. Livingstone. Oxford: Oxford University Press, 1997,

405–6. Two major standard works on Constantine include Timothy D. Barnes, *Constantine and Eusebius* (Cambridge: Harvard University Press, 1981), and A. H. M. Jones, *Constantine and the Conversion of Europe* (Toronto: University of Toronto Press, 2003).

Sadly, there is another story that could be told about the Christendom that emerged in the fourth century and beyond. The faith that had won the world through service and suffering was now, after Constantine, the beneficiary of power and privilege. With the Christianisation of the emperors, Christian morality slowly began to be written into law and so was thrust upon unbelievers. Bishops were given an elevated status and easy access to power—for a brief time, they were even made civic magistrates. Over the next two centuries—from, say, AD 350 to 550—church and state gradually became entwined.

By the fifth century, churches had acquired land and wealth way beyond their needs, and those who opposed Christ's cause found themselves excluded, silenced, and worse. Now the church grew, not through the inexplicable power of words and deeds but by the all too familiar means of warfare and treaty. Imperialism became the handmaiden of Christian mission, as an earthly "Christendom" became synonymous with God's kingdom. In the twinkling of an eye, it seems, the people of the Servant King had assumed a throne of their own.

It was by no means *all* bad—much exaggeration is offered about this period. And Christians can find consolation in the fact that for the first couple of centuries it was mostly very good, remarkable even! But, for me, the church of the fifth century and beyond provides ample proof that when Christians wield secular power for the cause of Christ, they frequently cease to be recognisably Christian. The only "power" the historical Jesus ever granted his followers was the power to *persuade* through word and service. As the famous Yale philosopher and theologian Miroslav Volf said on national TV in Australia when pressed about the issue of church and state:

> For the church to be marginal isn't that bad of a thing. Church was born as a marginal institution. For many centuries it stayed as a marginal institution and I think if we are detached from power, we can see things much more clearly, we can project authentic Christian vision much more—much better. I think it's healthy for the church to learn how to live from the margins and contribute from the margins to the wellbeing of society. ("Biennale, Babies and Blokes." ABC Q&A. http://www.abc .net.au/tv/qanda/txt/s3951334.htm.)

# EPILOGUE:
## PORTRAIT OF A FOLLOWER OF JESUS

Belonging to the movement inspired by the man from Nazareth begins with careful reflection on the many and varied portraits of him found in the earliest sources, the texts of the New Testament, and especially the Gospels. More than that, it involves allowing these images to have their intended effect. Following Jesus, then, means learning and applying the wisdom of the *Teacher*, alleviating suffering in the name of the *Healer*, and trying to live out one's imperfect life within the larger, perfect life of Jesus as the true *Israel*.

To be a Christian is also to bear the name (and shame) of the *Christ* and to revere him as the *Judge* of all injustice, including the injustice in me. At the same time, it is to approach him as the *Friend* of sinners, as the *Temple* of divine presence and mercy, and the *Saviour* who died for us all. So long as these portraits are held in careful balance—part of the fun and seriousness of the Christian life—true believers can never be smug in their righteousness or burdened by their unworthiness.

As the risen one Jesus is *Adam*, the progenitor of a new humanity and the guarantor of my own resurrection to eternal life. With this hope, I can sit loosely to the claims of my culture, knowing that all earthly empires pass into oblivion while the kingdom of the true *Caesar* reigns eternal.

Knowing Jesus, finally, involves embracing a scandalous paradox: the one in whose face we see *God* also declared himself to be the *Servant* of all. No belief is more counterintuitive or revolutionary. If it is true, it means that at the heart of the universe is One who values humility above status, service above power, and generosity above privilege. And if I truly believe this, nothing will ever be the same.

# Doubter's Guide to the Bible

## Inside History's Bestseller for Believers and Skeptics

*John Dickson*

*A Doubter's Guide to the Bible* is a concise account of the whole biblical narrative and the lifestyle it inspires, representing a unique and engaging framework for those observing Christianity from the outside, especially those who think there are good reasons not to believe.

In this book, Dickson provides a readable and winsome Bible primer summarizing the main themes in Scripture and addresses tough questions such as, "How can we read the creation account in Genesis in light of modern science?" and "How do we approach Old Testament law when it appears inconsistent and irrelevant?"

By presenting the whole of the Bible as an account of God's promise to restore humanity to himself, and humanity to one another and to creation, Dickson allows believers and skeptics alike to gain insight into why the Bible has been a compelling, life-changing, and magnetic force throughout the ages.

*Available in stores and online!*

**ZONDERVAN®**
.com

# A Doubter's Guide to the Ten Commandments

*John Dickson*

In *A Doubter's Guide to the Ten Commandments*, bestselling author John Dickson explores how these ten ancient instructions have changed our world and how they show us what the Good Life looks like. Whether or not one believes in the Bible, these ten ancient instructions open up a window to the Western world and on our own souls.

# Life of Jesus

## Who He Is and Why He Matters

*John Dickson*

What really happened back in the first century, in Jerusalem and around the Sea of Galilee, that changed the shape of world history? Who is this figure who emerges from history to have a profound impact on culture, ethics, politics, and philosophy? Join historian John Dickson on this journey through the life of Jesus.

This book, which features a self-contained discussion guide for use with *Life of Jesus* DVD (available separately), will help you and your friends dig deeper into what is known about Jesus' life and why it matters.

> "John Dickson has done a marvelous job of presenting the story of Jesus, and the full meaning of that story, in a way that is both deeply faithful to the biblical sources and refreshingly relevant to tomorrow's world and church. I strongly recommend this study to anyone who wants to re-examine the deep historical roots of Christian faith and to find them as life-giving as they ever were."—Tom Wright

*Available in stores and online!*

**ZONDERVAN®**
.com

# The Christ Files

## How Historians Know What They Know about Jesus

*John Dickson*

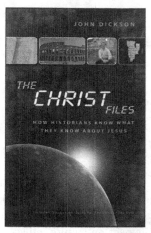

In *The Christ Files*, a four-session small group Bible study, John Dickson examines the Christian faith through a historical look at the Christian faith and life of Jesus from both scriptural and other non-biblical documentation.

Unique among the world's religions, the central claims of Christianity concern not just timeless spiritual truths but tangible historical events as well. Historian John Dickson examines Christianity's claims in the light of history, opening you and your group to a wealth of ancient sources and explaining how mainstream scholars—whether or not they claim Christian faith personally—reach their conclusions about history's most influential figure, Jesus of Nazareth.

*The Christ Files* will help you and your small group expand your understanding of early Christianity and the life of Jesus.

This 110-page participant guide includes seven chapters of reading and background information, along with questions for four impactful small group sessions. It is meant for use in conjunction with the four-session *The Christ Files* DVD (sold separately).

*Available in stores and online!*